Well Read 3

SKILLS AND STRATEGIES FOR READING

Mindy Pasternak | Elisaveta Wrangell

OXFORD
UNIVERSITY PRESS

OXFORD
UNIVERSITY PRESS

198 Madison Avenue
New York, NY 10016 USA

Great Clarendon Street, Oxford OX2 6DP UK

Oxford University Press is a department of the University of Oxford.
It furthers the University's objective of excellence in research, scholarship,
and education by publishing worldwide in

Oxford New York

Auckland Cape Town Dar es Salaam Hong Kong Karachi
Kuala Lumpur Madrid Melbourne Mexico City Nairobi
New Delhi Shanghai Taipei Toronto

With offices in

Argentina Austria Brazil Chile Czech Republic France Greece
Guatemala Hungary Italy Japan Poland Portugal Singapore
South Korea Switzerland Thailand Turkey Ukraine Vietnam

OXFORD and OXFORD ENGLISH are registered trademarks of
Oxford University Press

© Oxford University Press 2008

Database right Oxford University Press (maker)

Editorial Director: Sally Yagan
Senior Publishing Manager: Pietro Alongi
Design Project Manager: Maj Hagsted
Senior Designer: Claudia Carlson
Production Layout Artist: Julie Armstrong
Image Editor: Robin Fadool
Production Manager: Shanta Persaud
Production Controller: Eve Wong

ISBN: 978 0 19 476104 8

Printed in Hong Kong

10 9 8 7 6 5 4 3 2 1

ACKNOWLEDGMENTS

Cover art: Claudia Carlson

The publisher would like to thank the following for their permission to
reproduce copyright material: **pp. 4–5**, "Survival at Sea" Photo and story
courtesy of the U.S. Naval Safety Center. **pp. 9–10**, "The Only Way Out"
Shane Burrows, www.Climb-Utah.com. Reprinted by permission. **pp.
23–24**, "Evelyn Glennie, Solo Percussionist", Making Music, Silver Burdett.
Published by Scott Foresman. Copyright by Pearson Education.
pp. 31–32, Heidi Waleson, "Leader of the Pack," LiveMusic, Oct. 17, 1999.
Reprinted by permission of Minnesota Orchestra. **pp. 38–40**, "Study
Concludes Beethoven Died from Lead Poisoning" by Rick Weiss. © 2006,
The Washington Post, reprinted with permission. **pp. 47–48**, Michael Hill,
"Despite the Growing Popularity of 'Food Culture,' Many Can't Cook,"
Associated Press, Jul 10, 2005. **p. 52**, Food Faux Pas By Terri Morrison,
Excerpted from OAG Frequent Flyer, July 9, 2003. Reprinted by permission
of Terri Morrison. **pp. 59–60**, Stephen Jack, Deliciously Malodorous, www.
eatingchina.com. Reprinted by permission. **p. 67**, "Sand Castles—Amazing
Design, Temporary Art" First published in Block Island Times. Used by per-
mission. **pp. 73–74**, Will Marquand, White Heat, Kansai Time Out, January
2005. Reprinted by permission of Kansai Time Out. **pp. 81–83**, CNN, From
Graffiti to Galleries, CNN.com, November 4, 2005. **p. 91**, "Swimming with
the Fishes: Slabs of the Old Wilson Bridge Find New Life as a Bay Reef" by
Megan Greenwell. © 2006, The Washington Post, reprinted with permission. **pp. 96–97**, "Ghanaian Helps Disabled Countrymen" by Miki Farley.
Copyright © 2004 by Western Media LLC. Reprinted and adapted with
permission. **pp. 105–107**, Ko Shu-ling, Taiwan's own 'Forrest Gump' turns
his focus from the South Pole to the Sahara, March 20, 2006 (http://www.
taipeitimes.com/News/taiwan/archives/2006/03/20/2003298257). Reprinted
by permission of Taipei Times. **p. 122**, "Fooled for Love" Produced by
ScienCentral, Inc. Funded in part by the National Science Foundation
under Grant No. ESI-0206184. **pp. 130–131**, "Seahorse Fathers Take Reins
in Childbirth" Courtesy National Geographic News, www.nationalgeo-
graphic.com/news. **pp. 140–141**, David Adam, "T-rex Could Bring Jurassic
Park to Life: Scientists say dinosaur cloning possible from DNA," The
Guardian, March 25, 2005. Copyright Guardian News & Media Ltd 2005. **pp.
146–148**, Jonathan Silverstein, "Organ Printing" Could Drastically Change
Medicine, Feb 10, 2006, ABCNews.com. Used by permission of ABC News.
pp. 154–155, Ancient Surgery, www.channel4.com **p. 163**, "Addicted to
the Internet" Material reprinted with the express permission of CANWEST
NEWS SERVICE, a CanWest Partnership. **pp. 167–168**, Cassie Shaner,
Exercise addiction affects campuses, Daily Athanaeum, March 10, 2004
pp. 175–177, April Frawley Birdwell, "Addicted to phones? Cell phone use
becoming a major problem for some, expert says," University of Florida.
Used by permission of April Frawley Birdwell.

The authors and publisher would like to acknowledge the following indi-
viduals for their invaluable input during the development of this series:
Macarena Aguilar, Cy-Fair College, TX; Sharon Allerson, East Los Angeles
College, CA; Susan Niemeyer, Los Angeles City College, CA; Elaine S. Paris,
Koc University, Istanbul, Turkey; Sylvia Cavazos Pena, University of Texas
at Brownsville, TX; Maggy Sami Saba, King Abdulaziz University, Jeddah,
Kingdom of Saudi Arabia; Stephanie Toland, North Side Learning Center,
MN; Jay Myoung Yu, Yonsei University at Wonju, Korea; Anthony Zak,
Universitas Sam Ratulangi, Manado, Indonesia.

Special thanks go to Barbara Rifkind for her support of the editorial team.

AUTHOR ACKNOWLEDGMENTS

We express our sincere thanks to Peggy Cleve, without whose prompting
and guidance, this series would not have been written. We also thank our
families and the following friends and colleagues for their encouragement,
advice, and support: H. Douglas Brown, Wendy Crockett, Sheila Dwight,
François Hervé, Lee Egerman, Paolo Longoni, Dave Myers, Don Orf, Patricia
Porter, and Deborah vanDommelen. We are furthermore grateful to the
students at the University of California, Riverside's International Education
Programs for their invaluable input in the development of this series. Finally,
we thank Phebe Szatmari and Pietro Alongi, and the Oxford University Press
editorial and design staff for their hard work on this series.

Notes to the Teacher

Welcome to *Well Read*, a four-level series that teaches and reinforces crucial reading skills and vocabulary strategies step-by-step through a wide range of authentic texts that are meant to engage students' (and teachers') interest. *Well Read 3* is intended for students at the intermediate level.

Each of the eight chapters in the book revolves around a central theme, but every text in a chapter approaches the theme from a different angle or level of formality. This provides multiple insights into the subject matter, while at the same time developing reading skills. Thus, students will be able to approach the theme with increasing fluency.

Well Read is designed so that all the activities, including reading, are broken up into smaller pieces, and each has specific goals so that all students, regardless of their individual level, can participate and succeed. The activities in the book support the approach that students do *not* have to understand every word of a text in order to understand its basic themes. Vocabulary strategies in each chapter allow students to feel more comfortable guessing the meanings of unfamiliar words or phrases based on their context.

Chapter Introduction

The opening page introduces the chapter's theme. The questions and photographs are designed to activate the students' prior knowledge, as well as stimulate some limited discussion before the previewing, reading, and post-reading activities.

Getting Started

This activity precedes each text or graphic component. It is designed to help students focus in on a more specific topic through reflection and discussion. It also introduces a small number of critical vocabulary words or phrases.

Active Previewing

Active Previewing asks students to read only brief and selected parts of the text, and then answer very simple questions that focus on this material. This activity encourages the notion that students do not have to understand each and every word of what they are reading. There is a strong emphasis on how to preview a wide range of genres, both academic and non-academic, including—but not limited to—newspaper articles, online texts, magazine articles, textbook articles, tables, charts, graphs, timelines, and graphics.

Reading and Recalling

The first reading activity asks students to read and recall. This approach is less daunting than being presented with an entire text, and also allows the students to retain more. Recalling encourages students to be accountable for the material they read. At its most basic, students build their short-term memories. On a deeper level, students begin to process information more quickly and holistically. Perfect recall is never the goal.

Understanding the Text

After each text, students are presented with a two-part reading comprehension activity. The first part checks the students' comprehension of the most basic ideas expressed in the text, whereas the second part challenges the students to recall other key ideas and information.

Reading Skills

Students are introduced to topic, main idea, and supporting details in separate chapters, which allows them to practice and master each of these skills before progressing to the next. Earlier chapters present choices in a multiple choice fashion, whereas subsequent chapters require the students to write their own interpretations. The ability to think critically about the information that is presented in the text is a crucial part of being an active reader.

Vocabulary Strategies

Students first learn that they can understand the general idea of a text without understanding every word; however, skipping words is not always an option. Therefore, throughout the book, students are introduced to different strategies that can help them determine the meanings of new vocabulary without using their dictionaries. The various vocabulary strategies are presented and then reinforced in later chapters. All vocabulary activities present the vocabulary as it is used in the texts themselves, yet the vocabulary strategies that are taught can be applied universally to reading that the students do outside class. Developing these strategies will allow students to become more autonomous readers.

Discussing the Issues

Every text ends with a series of questions that encourage the students to express their opinions and ideas about the general subject discussed in the text. The questions are designed to be communicative in that they strike upon compelling issues raised in the text.

Putting It On Paper

Reading and writing are two skills that inherently go together. The writing activity complements the chapter texts, yet it is also designed to stand independently should the teacher decide not to read all of the chapter texts. Each *Putting It On Paper* activity offers two writing prompts; the teacher can allow students to choose between the prompts or can select one prompt for all students to use.

Taking It Online

Each *Taking It Online* activity guides the students through the steps necessary for conducting online research, based on the theme of the chapter. Teachers might opt to prescreen a select number of websites in advance, thus directing the students to more reliable and useful sites. *Taking It Online* finishes with a follow-up activity that enables the students to take their research one step further, in pairs or groups.

An Answer Key, a PowerPoint® Teaching Tool, and an ExamView Assessment Suite® Test Generator with customizable tests and quizzes are also available with each level of *Well Read* in the *Well Read Instructor's Pack*.

Contents

Welcome to *Well Read*

Well Read 3 is the third level in a four-level reading series that strategically develops students' reading skills, setting them up for success as critical thinkers.

There are eight chapters in *Well Read* and seven sections in each chapter: *Chapter Introduction, Text 1, Text 2, Text 3, Text 4, Putting It On Paper,* and *Taking It Online.*

Chapter Introduction

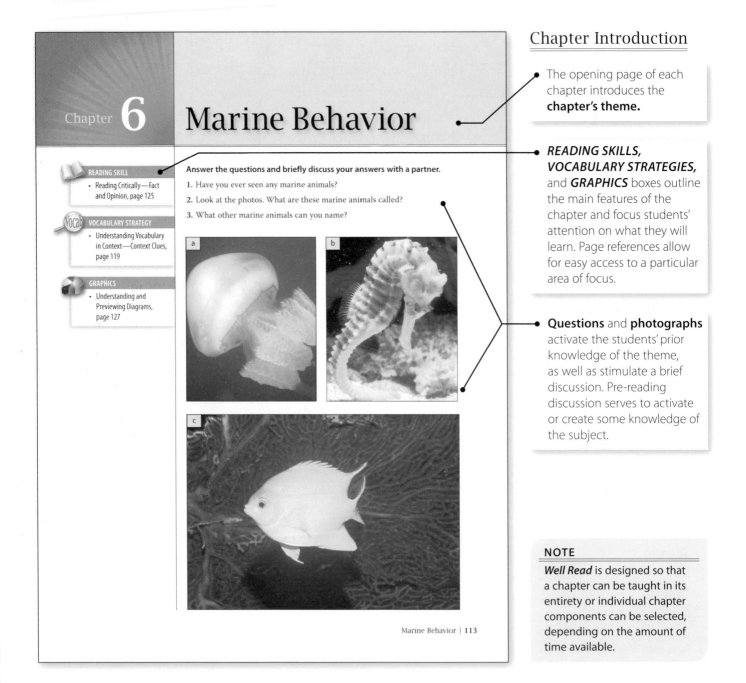

The opening page of each chapter introduces the **chapter's theme.**

READING SKILLS, VOCABULARY STRATEGIES, and *GRAPHICS* boxes outline the main features of the chapter and focus students' attention on what they will learn. Page references allow for easy access to a particular area of focus.

Questions and **photographs** activate the students' prior knowledge of the theme, as well as stimulate a brief discussion. Pre-reading discussion serves to activate or create some knowledge of the subject.

NOTE

Well Read is designed so that a chapter can be taught in its entirety or individual chapter components can be selected, depending on the amount of time available.

The content within the illustrated chapter page:

Chapter **6** **Marine Behavior**

READING SKILL
• Reading Critically—Fact and Opinion, page 125

VOCABULARY STRATEGY
• Understanding Vocabulary in Context—Context Clues, page 119

GRAPHICS
• Understanding and Previewing Diagrams, page 127

Answer the questions and briefly discuss your answers with a partner.

1. Have you ever seen any marine animals?
2. Look at the photos. What are these marine animals called?
3. What other marine animals can you name?

Marine Behavior | 113

Text 1 | Danger in the Sea

1 | Getting Started

A. Answer the questions and briefly discuss your answers with a partner.

1. Have you ever been stung by an animal or insect?

2. What can happen if you are stung?

3. What are some animal and insect stings that can be deadly?

B. Look at the photos and fill in the chart on the next page.

a

b

c

d

e

2 | Active Previewing

Preview the magazine article on the next page. Underline the title, the first sentence of each paragraph, and the last sentence of the text as you preview. Then answer the questions with a partner.

1. What is the topic of this text?

2. What is the main idea of this text?

2 | Skimming

A. Skim the online article below in four minutes or less. Then answer the questions with a partner.

1. According to the text, what do scientists think they will be able to do one day?

2. What do scientists use to do the technology mentioned in the text?

3. What is one name for the new technology?

4. Has the technology been perfected yet?

REMEMBER
Skimming a text will help you identify the topic and main idea. There is no need for a separate preview.

Getting Started

- Before each text, students **anticipate the more specific topic**—as opposed to the more generalized theme of the chapter.

- A small number of **critical vocabulary words or phrases** are introduced.

Active Previewing and Skimming

- Students are taught how to **actively** preview a wide range of genres, both academic and non-academic, including newspaper articles, online texts, magazine articles, textbook articles, and graphics (see **Graphics** on page xii).

- The skill of **skimming** a text for general meaning is also introduced in later chapters, at which point, there is no need to do a separate preview of a text.

Text 1, 2, and 4

The **texts** progress in length and level of difficulty in each chapter, and they are **authentic** in both presentation and content. Genres include: online texts, newspaper articles, magazine articles, and textbook articles, among others.

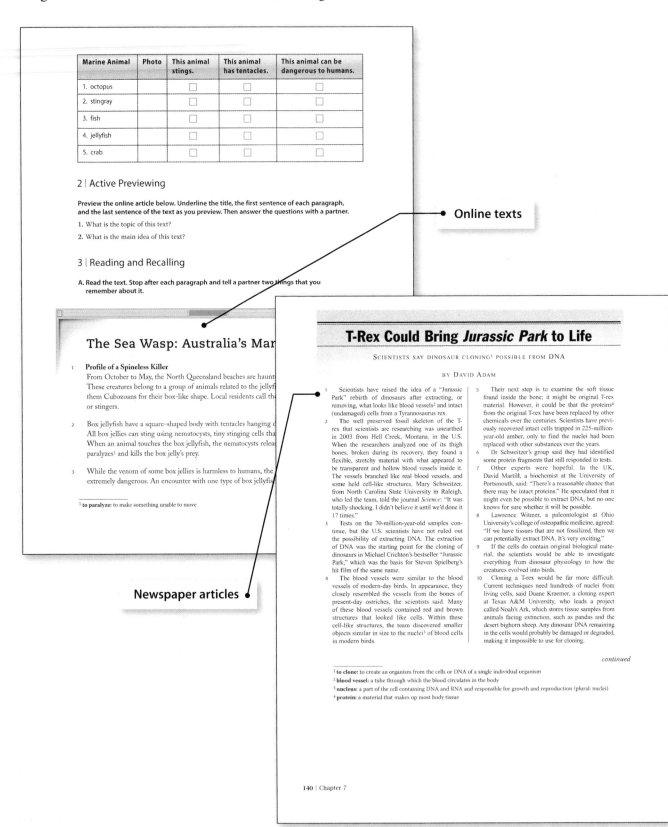

Marine Animal	Photo	This animal stings.	This animal has tentacles.	This animal can be dangerous to humans.
1. octopus		☐	☐	☐
2. stingray		☐	☐	☐
3. fish		☐	☐	☐
4. jellyfish		☐	☐	☐
5. crab		☐	☐	☐

2 | Active Previewing

Preview the online article below. Underline the title, the first sentence of each paragraph, and the last sentence of the text as you preview. Then answer the questions with a partner.

1. What is the topic of this text?
2. What is the main idea of this text?

3 | Reading and Recalling

A. Read the text. Stop after each paragraph and tell a partner two things that you remember about it.

Online texts

The Sea Wasp: Australia's Mar

1   **Profile of a Spineless Killer**
From October to May, the North Queensland beaches are haunt
These creatures belong to a group of animals related to the jellyf
them Cubozoans for their box-like shape. Local residents call the
or stingers.

2   Box jellyfish have a square-shaped body with tentacles hanging
All box jellies can sting using nematocysts, tiny stinging cells tha
When an animal touches the box jellyfish, the nematocysts releas
paralyzes[1] and kills the box jelly's prey.

3   While the venom of some box jellies is harmless to humans, the
extremely dangerous. An encounter with one type of box jellyfis

---
[1] **to paralyze:** to make something unable to move

Newspaper articles

T-Rex Could Bring *Jurassic Park* to Life

SCIENTISTS SAY DINOSAUR CLONING[1] POSSIBLE FROM DNA

BY DAVID ADAM

1   Scientists have raised the idea of a "Jurassic Park" rebirth of dinosaurs after extracting, or removing, what looks like blood vessels[2] and intact (undamaged) cells from a Tyrannosaurus rex.

2   The well preserved fossil skeleton of the T-rex that scientists are researching was unearthed in 2003 from Hell Creek, Montana, in the U.S. When the researchers analyzed one of its thigh bones, broken during its recovery, they found a flexible, stretchy material with what appeared to be transparent and hollow blood vessels inside it. The vessels branched like real blood vessels, and some held cell-like structures. Mary Schweitzer, from North Carolina State University in Raleigh, who led the team, told the journal *Science*: "It was totally shocking. I didn't believe it until we'd done it 17 times."

3   Tests on the 70-million-year-old samples continue, but the U.S. scientists have not ruled out the possibility of extracting DNA. The extraction of DNA is the starting point for the cloning of dinosaurs in Michael Crichton's bestseller "Jurassic Park," which was the basis for Steven Spielberg's hit film of the same name.

4   The blood vessels were similar to the blood vessels of modern-day birds. In appearance, they closely resembled the vessels from the bones of present-day ostriches, the scientists said. Many of these blood vessels contained red and brown structures that looked like cells. Within these cell-like structures, the team discovered smaller objects similar in size to the nuclei[3] of blood cells in modern birds.

5   Their next step is to examine the soft tissue found inside the bone; it might be original T-rex material. However, it could be that the proteins[4] from the original T-rex have been replaced by other chemicals over the centuries. Scientists have previously recovered intact cells trapped in 225-million-year-old amber, only to find the nuclei had been replaced with other substances over the years.

6   Dr Schweitzer's group said they had identified some protein fragments that still responded to tests.

7   Other experts were hopeful. In the UK, David Martill, a biochemist at the University of Portsmouth, said: "There's a reasonable chance that there may be intact proteins." He speculated that it might even be possible to extract DNA, but no one knows for sure whether it will be possible.

8   Lawrence Witmer, a paleontologist at Ohio University's college of osteopathic medicine, agreed: "If we have tissues that are not fossilized, then we can potentially extract DNA. It's very exciting."

9   If the cells do contain original biological material, the scientists would be able to investigate everything from dinosaur physiology to how the creatures evolved into birds.

10   Cloning a T-rex would be far more difficult. Current techniques need hundreds of nuclei from living cells, said Duane Kraemer, a cloning expert at Texas A&M University, who leads a project called Noah's Ark, which stores tissue samples from animals facing extinction, such as pandas and the desert bighorn sheep. Any dinosaur DNA remaining in the cells would probably be damaged or degraded, making it impossible to use for cloning.

continued

---
[1] **to clone:** to create an organism from the cells or DNA of a single individual organism
[2] **blood vessel:** a tube through which the blood circulates in the body
[3] **nucleus:** a part of the cell containing DNA and RNA and responsible for growth and reproduction (plural: nuclei)
[4] **protein:** a material that makes up most body tissue

140 | Chapter 7

A. Read the text. Stop after each paragraph and tell a partner two things that you remember about it.

Fooled for Love

The male australian cuttlefish sometimes has to disguise himself as a female if he wants to get a date.

1 "The male cuttlefish has quite a challenge on his hands when it comes to the end of [his] yearly life cycle," explains Roger Hanlon, senior scientist at the Marine Biological Laboratory. "There are four, five, even ten males for every female on the spawning grounds. Therefore, the challenge each male cuttlefish faces is how to get its genes[1] into the next generation[2] of cuttlefish. Due to the low number of females, there is enormous competition among the males on the spawning grounds."

2 Rather than study fish close to home, Hanlon and his team spent five seasons observing cuttlefish underwater in a remote coastal area of Australia. As one might expect, the largest males used the advantage of their size to find a female partner and to guard[3] her from other males. However, Hanlon observed with interest that smaller males were able to get to the female while the guard male was fighting other males away, or by meeting the female in a "secret rendezvous[4]" under a rock.

3 Hanlon found that the small males with the biggest success rate use a special trick. They change their skin pattern and body shape to disguise themselves as females. Then they are able to swim right past a large guard male, who thinks he's getting another girlfriend. Hanlon explains that these smaller males do not try to fight the larger males because they must know instinctually that they cannot win.

4 While the larger males have a more direct approach, many of the smaller males use a sneaky approach, according to Hanlon. The small male cuttlefish will hide his fourth set of arms (females have only three sets), swell his arms up—as if he is carrying an egg—and change his skin coloration to a pattern that is usual in females. Then he just swims right past the large guard male. "And every single time that this happens," says Hanlon, "the big male looks and thinks he's acquiring another female mate and he lets 'him/her' just swim right in next to the female." Once the small male is next to the female, he can attempt a mating.

5 Hanlon reported in the journal *Nature* that although females rejected 70 percent of mating attempts overall, they accepted the majority[5] of advances from the mimics, or disguised males. The female cuttlefish collects sperm from several males. It is not until later that she uses some of it to fertilize her eggs. Hanlon also found that the females often used the mimics' sperm to fertilize their eggs. So mating in and of itself does not necessarily lead to fertilization. By using a genetic test called DNA fingerprinting, Hanlon found that the female more often than not fertilized her next egg with sperm from the mimic.

6 "[The female cuttlefish is] rejecting 70 percent of mating attempts, yet she's taking these small mimics at a much higher rate," Hanlon says. "Why is that? We don't know the answer, but there's something attractive, clever, some sign of fitness." He believes that perhaps the cleverness of the small mimic cuttlefish is an indirect sign of good genes in that animal. Therefore, the female will take the gamble of mating w[...] that he's a good match for he[...]

---

[1] **gene:** a basic biological unit that passes on characteristics from parent to child
[2] **generation:** here, the group of cuttlefish that will be born to the present group of cuttlefish
[3] **to guard:** to protect
[4] **rendezvous:** meeting
[5] **majority:** the greater number

Magazine articles

Textbook articles

Seahorse Fathers Take Reins[1] in Childbirth

1 It is true that male seahorses never play ball with their children or help them with their homework. But they do outdo human dads in one way: male seahorses go through pregnancy and give birth to their sons and daughters. This ability is unique to these strange and fascinating fish that live and reproduce in tropical and mild coastal waters worldwide.

2 Seahorses, which range from less than one inch up to a foot (from one to 30 centimeters) in length, have evolved a number of unusual adaptations[2]—a special tail that can hold on to underwater plants, a tubelike mouth for sucking in tiny sea animals, and protective bony plates in their skin. There are 32 species, or kinds, of seahorses, all belonging to the genus *Hippocampus*.

3 "They're such an unusual-looking fish, people sometimes don't realize they're real fish," said Alison Scarratt, in charge of fishes at the National Aquarium in Baltimore. Due to special bony plates that cover its body, the seahorse is unpalatable, or unpleasant to eat, to most predators. However, its survival is endangered by human predators, who hunt the seahorse especially for use in traditional medicines.

4 No statistical data on seahorse populations is available because relatively little research on seahorses has been done until recently. According to a network[3] of scientists from various institutions, fishers have reported a decrease in the number and size of seahorses they catch. These scientists conduct research under a program called Project Seahorse. The goal of this program is to find marine conservation solutions while using the seahorse as its main focus.

5 Although seahorses are easily able to breed[4] in their natural environment, breeding seahorses in captivity has been a problem, in part because the babies are so tiny that it is hard to keep them alive with the available feeding techniques. The marine scientists in Baltimore are working to develop effective methods that will help ensure the creature's survival.

6 **Male Birth**

The male seahorse carries as many as 2,000 babies in a pouch on the outside of its stomach. A pregnancy lasts from 10 to 25 days, depending on the species.

7 The reproductive process begins when a male and a female seahorse do daily dances, intertwining their tails and swimming together. Eventually they engage in a true courtship[5] dance, which can last as long as eight hours. It ends with the female placing her eggs in the male's pouch. "Their mating ritual is quite beautiful," said Sarah Foster, a research biologist at McGill University in Montreal who is involved in Project Seahorse. Scientists think these movements have developed over time so that the male can receive the eggs when the female is ready to deposit them.

8 The eggs are then fertilized in the dad's pouch, and they also hatch in the pouch. The father cares for the young as they grow, controlling the water salinity, or saltiness, in the pouch to prepare them for life in the sea. When the tiny seahorses are ready to be born, the male expels the young from the pouch into the ocean.

9 **Cutting the Ties**

While seahorse dads do more than most dads by giving birth, seahorse parents do not provide their tiny offspring (children) with any care or protection after they are born. Infant seahorses often die by being eaten by predators or by being carried away by ocean currents.

10 Fewer than five infant seahorses in every 1,000 survive to adulthood, which helps explain why so many babies are born at the same time, said James Anderson, manager of the seahorse

continued

---

[1] **to take the reins:** to take control
[2] **adaptation:** here, a change in a species that improves its ability to interact with its environment
[3] **network:** a group
[4] **to breed:** to reproduce, to have children
[5] **courtship:** preparation for mating

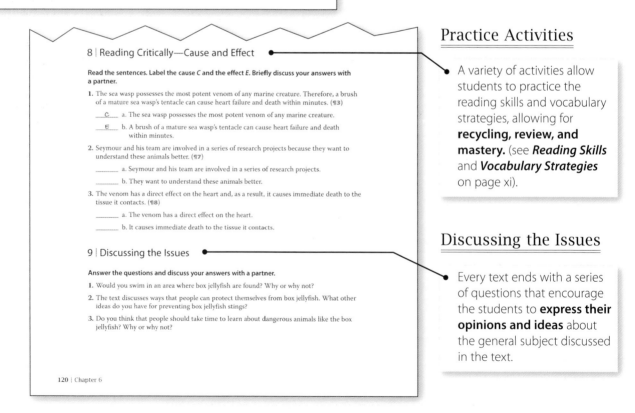

B. Read the text again without pausing. Tell your partner two new things that you remember.

C. Work as a class or in large groups. Try to name as many things as you can about the text.

4 | Understanding the Text

A. Answer as many questions as you can without looking at the text. Discuss your answers with a partner.

1. What marine animal is described in the text? _____

2. How does this animal sting its prey? _____

3. If a person is stung by this animal, what could happen to him or her? _____

B. Check (✔) the statement that best describes the animal discussed in the text.

It ...
☐ 1. ... has a square, translucent body with long tentacles hanging down from the corners.
☐ 2. ... is a large, fast-swimming river fish with two eyes.
☐ 3. ... is a flying insect, similar to a wasp or bee, with three eyes.

5 | Understanding the Topic, Main Idea, and Supporting Details

A. **Text.** Answer the questions and write *T* for *Topic*, *G* for *Too General*, and *S* for *Too Specific*. Discuss your answers with a partner.

1. What is the topic of the text? _____

2. Is your answer for the topic here the same as the one you determined after you previewed the text, or is your answer different? _____

3. What is the main idea of the text?

   a. _____ The sea wasp has long tentacles covered in nematocysts.

   b. _____ The sea wasp is a very venomous marine animal.

   c. _____ There are many venomous marine animals.

4. Is your answer for the main idea here the same as the one you determined after you previewed the text, or is your answer different? _____

8 | Reading Critically—Cause and Effect

Read the sentences. Label the cause *C* and the effect *E*. Briefly discuss your answers with a partner.

1. The sea wasp possesses the most potent venom of any marine creature. Therefore, a brush of a mature sea wasp's tentacle can cause heart failure and death within minutes. (¶3)

   ___C___ a. The sea wasp possesses the most potent venom of any marine creature.

   ___E___ b. A brush of a mature sea wasp's tentacle can cause heart failure and death within minutes.

2. Seymour and his team are involved in a series of research projects because they want to understand these animals better. (¶7)

   _____ a. Seymour and his team are involved in a series of research projects.

   _____ b. They want to understand these animals better.

3. The venom has a direct effect on the heart and, as a result, it causes immediate death to the tissue it contacts. (¶8)

   _____ a. The venom has a direct effect on the heart.

   _____ b. It causes immediate death to the tissue it contacts.

9 | Discussing the Issues

Answer the questions and discuss your answers with a partner.

1. Would you swim in an area where box jellyfish are found? Why or why not?

2. The text discusses ways that people can protect themselves from box jellyfish. What other ideas do you have for preventing box jellyfish stings?

3. Do you think that people should take time to learn about dangerous animals like the box jellyfish? Why or why not?

Understanding the Text

After each text, students are presented with a **two-part reading comprehension activity**. The first part checks the students' comprehension of the most basic ideas expressed in the text, whereas the second part challenges the students to recall other key ideas and information. Students are asked to complete as much as they can without looking back at the text.

Understanding the Topic, Main Idea, and Supporting Details

Topic, Main Idea, and *Supporting Details* are introduced in separate chapters, allowing for **practice and mastery** before progressing to the next skill. Earlier chapters present choices in a **multiple choice format**, whereas subsequent chapters require the students to **write their own interpretations**.

Practice Activities

A variety of activities allow students to practice the reading skills and vocabulary strategies, allowing for **recycling, review, and mastery.** (see *Reading Skills* and *Vocabulary Strategies* on page xi).

Discussing the Issues

Every text ends with a series of questions that encourage the students to **express their opinions and ideas** about the general subject discussed in the text.

Reading Skills

READING SKILL Reading Critically—Fact and Opinion

A **fact** is something that is true about a subject and can be tested or proven.

Read the following sentence.

There are four, five, even ten males for every female on the spawning grounds. (¶1)

Although the number of males to females varies, the fact that there are more males than females can be proven through documentation.

An **opinion** is what someone thinks about a subject. Opinions may be based on facts, but they show a person's feelings about something and cannot be tested or proven.

Read the following sentence.

The male cuttlefish has quite a *challenge* on his hands when it comes to the end of [his] yearly life cycle. (¶1)

The word *challenge* cannot be tested or proven. We cannot measure objectively whether the male cuttlefish considers this situation challenging or not. It is only the speaker's opinion that this situation is challenging to the males.

Marine Behavior | 125

- In each chapter, students are introduced to **new reading skills** and **vocabulary strategies**. They are always followed by a practice activity.

- The reading skills include *Active Previewing, Skimming, Scanning, Making Inferences,* and *Understanding the Topic, Main Idea,* and *Supporting Details,* among others.

Vocabulary Strategies

Vocab VOCABULARY STRATEGY Understanding Vocabulary in Context— Context Clues

Sometimes, we can understand the meaning of unfamiliar words by looking at the word(s) in the **context** of the sentences and paragraphs that surround them. To understand words through context clues:

1. Figure out the part of speech of the unfamiliar word(s).

2. Look at the surrounding information. See if this information contains clues about the meaning of the unfamiliar word(s).

3. Guess the meaning of the words using context clues to help you.

Read the following sentence.

In time, the number of *casualties* from box jellyfish may be reduced to zero. (¶10)

Who or what is a *casualty*? First, try to figure out the part of speech. The text is talking about a *number of* something, so *casualties* must be a noun. Next, look at the surrounding information. This paragraph talks about how people can protect themselves from box jellyfish, and this sentence discusses reducing something over time. We also know from the text that the main danger of box jellyfish is that they can sting and kill people. Therefore, we can guess that *casualties* means either *people who are killed by box jellyfish* or *stings*. We are left with two options. At this point, we have enough information to keep reading.

7 | Understanding Vocabulary in Context

A. Context Clues. Select the best meaning for each word or phrase according to the text. Discuss your answers with a partner.

1. venom (¶2)
   a. animal
   b. poison
   c. box jellyfish
2. prey (¶2)
   a. victim, animal that becomes food
   b. baby, child
   c. cell
3. fatal (¶3)
   a. deadly
   b. safe
   c. short

4. potent (¶3)
   a. comfortable
   b. powerful
   c. quick
5. brush (¶3)
   a. taste
   b. touch
   c. smell

Marine Behavior | 119

- Students are introduced to a variety of vocabulary strategies that can help them determine the meanings of new vocabulary **without using their dictionaries**.

- All vocabulary strategies present the vocabulary as it is used in the texts themselves, **in context**, yet the strategies themselves **can be applied universally** to reading that students do outside class.

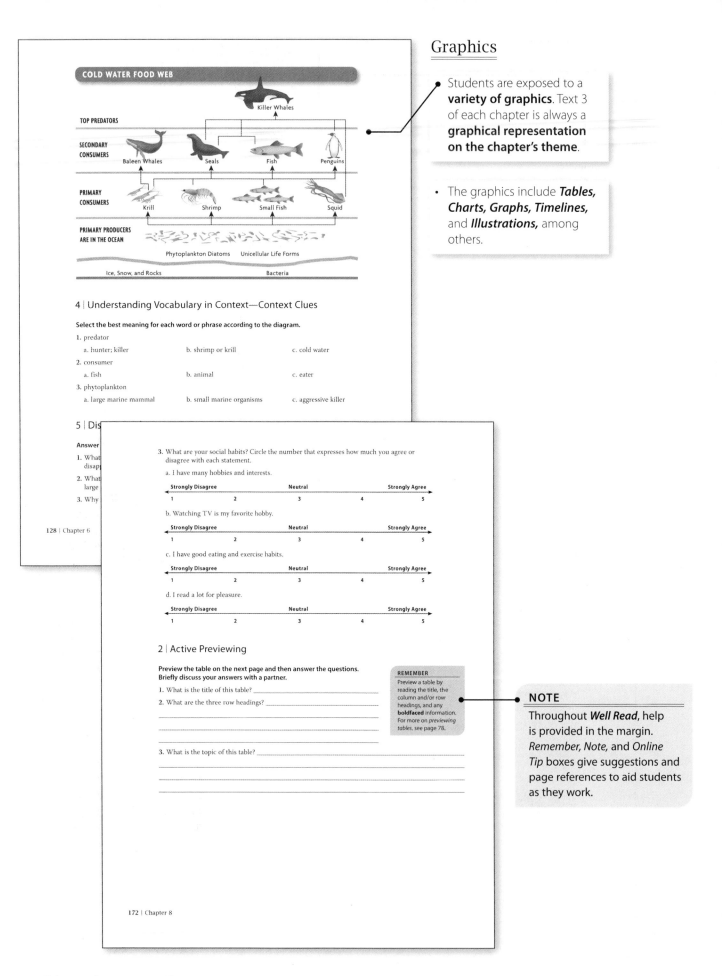

Graphics

- Students are exposed to a **variety of graphics**. Text 3 of each chapter is always a **graphical representation on the chapter's theme**.

- The graphics include **Tables, Charts, Graphs, Timelines,** and **Illustrations,** among others.

COLD WATER FOOD WEB

Killer Whales

TOP PREDATORS

SECONDARY CONSUMERS
Baleen Whales   Seals   Fish   Penguins

PRIMARY CONSUMERS
Krill   Shrimp   Small Fish   Squid

PRIMARY PRODUCERS ARE IN THE OCEAN

Phytoplankton Diatoms   Unicellular Life Forms

Ice, Snow, and Rocks   Bacteria

4 | Understanding Vocabulary in Context—Context Clues

Select the best meaning for each word or phrase according to the diagram.

1. predator
   a. hunter; killer   b. shrimp or krill   c. cold water

2. consumer
   a. fish   b. animal   c. eater

3. phytoplankton
   a. large marine mammal   b. small marine organisms   c. aggressive killer

5 | Dis

Answer

1. What
disapp

2. What
large

3. Why

3. What are your social habits? Circle the number that expresses how much you agree or disagree with each statement.

   a. I have many hobbies and interests.

Strongly Disagree		Neutral		Strongly Agree
1	2	3	4	5

   b. Watching TV is my favorite hobby.

Strongly Disagree		Neutral		Strongly Agree
1	2	3	4	5

   c. I have good eating and exercise habits.

Strongly Disagree		Neutral		Strongly Agree
1	2	3	4	5

   d. I read a lot for pleasure.

Strongly Disagree		Neutral		Strongly Agree
1	2	3	4	5

2 | Active Previewing

Preview the table on the next page and then answer the questions. Briefly discuss your answers with a partner.

1. What is the title of this table? _____

2. What are the three row headings? _____
_____
_____

3. What is the topic of this table? _____
_____
_____
_____

REMEMBER
Preview a table by reading the title, the column and/or row headings, and any **boldfaced** information. For more on *previewing tables*, see page 78.

NOTE

Throughout **Well Read**, help is provided in the margin. *Remember, Note,* and *Online Tip* boxes give suggestions and page references to aid students as they work.

Putting It On Paper

A. Write a paragraph on one of these topics.

1. What could happen if some ocean species disappear?

2. How can research on marine animals affect the survival of a species?

Steps for your paragraph

a. In your first sentence, clearly state your opinion about the topic.

b. In your supporting sentences, use details that support your opinion.

c. Be sure to include at least one cause and one effect in your paragraph.

B. Exchange paragraphs with a partner. First, read your partner's paragraph and answer the questions in the checklist. Then give feedback to your partner.

✔ CHECKLIST
1. Does the first sentence clearly show which topic your partner chose?
2. Do the following sentences give examples that support or illustrate the topic?
3. Does the paragraph show clearly your partner's point of view about his or her topic?
4. Does the paragraph contain at least one cause and one effect?
5. Is there any information in the paragraph that is not related to your partner's topic? If yes, please underline it on your partner's paper, and write it below:

_____

_____

_____

_____

_____

_____

_____

C. Revis

Taking It Online | Ocean Life

A. With a partner, use the Internet to research two marine animals.

1. Use Google (www.google.com) or another major search engine to find Websites with information about two of the following marine animals:

bottlenose dolphin	humpback whale	octopus
giant clam	moray eel	sea turtle

2. Preview the Websites.

> **ONLINE TIP**
> Use quotation marks in the search box to search for word groups or phrases:
> "moray eel"
> "octopus fact"
> "sea turtles eat"

B. Complete the tables with the information you find.

Marine animal:	sea otter
Website address(es): http://www.enchantedlearning.com	
Where are they found? Pacific Ocean coasts, bays, and kelp beds	
What do they eat? crabs, clams, mussels, octopuses, squid, sea urchins, fish, etc.	
What predators do they have (if any)? some sharks and birds	
One interesting fact about this animal: They don't have any fat to keep them warm. Instead, they have the densest fur of all mammals.	

Marine animal:	
Website address(es):	
Where are they found?	
What do they eat?	
What predators do they have (if any)?	
One interesting fact about this animal:	

Marine animal:	
Website address(es):	
Where are they found?	
What do they eat?	
What predators do they have (if any)?	
One interesting fact about this animal:	

C. Following up. Draw a food web for one of your marine animals. Compare it with the food web of a classmate who researched the same animal. Are your food webs similar?

136 | Chapter 6

Putting It On Paper

- In each chapter, students have the opportunity to write a **paragraph, letter,** or **essay** based on the chapter's theme.

- The writing activity complements the chapter texts, yet it is also **designed to stand independently** if all of the chapter texts are not covered.

Each *Putting It On Paper* activity offers **two writing prompts**.

Taking It Online

- Every chapter culminates with a *Taking It Online* activity. This activity guides students through the steps necessary for **conducting online research**, based on the theme of the chapter.

- The online activity is **open** to the extent that students are encouraged to find their own sites, **but it is also focused** enough so that students will not be roaming through undirected data.

Taking It Online finishes with a **follow-up activity** that enables students to **take their research one step further**, in pairs or groups.

Survival Psychology

Answer the questions and briefly discuss your answers with a partner.

1. Look at the photos. Are any of these activities dangerous?

2. What activity does each photo show?

3. What kinds of people like these activities? Why do they like them?

Text 1 | Swimming for Her Life

1 | Getting Started

A. Circle all of the activities you have done.

swimming in the ocean

treading water

flying in a small plane

B. Answer the questions and briefly discuss your answers with a partner.

1. Why is it important to know how to tread water? To swim?

2. Have you been trained for an emergency situation? Explain.

3. What could happen if people are not calm in an emergency?

When reading a text, you may encounter unfamiliar words or phrases. One good strategy is to **skip them**. They may not be necessary to understand the meaning of a paragraph or the meaning of the whole text.

However, if you find that a paragraph is unclear when you skip words or phrases:

1. Figure out the part of speech of the words or phrases you skipped (noun, adjective, verb, adverb).

2. Think about what you do understand.

3. Keep reading.

Read the following sentence.

Three miles from the xxxx, the engine of the plane stopped.

First, try to figure out the part of speech. The article *the* suggests that the skipped word is a noun: *Three miles from the* "something," *the engine of the plane stopped.* Think about what you *do* understand (that the engine of the plane stopped three miles from something the plane could land on), and keep reading.

2 | Skipping Words and Phrases

A. Read the sentences and cross out the words you do not understand. Then write their parts of speech on the blanks.

1. To save time, Maready decided not to file a flight plan.

_____

2. She landed so smoothly and easily that the plane's emergency-locator transmitter (ELT) was not activated.

_____

3. Maready tried to retrieve her scuba gear, but the bag was stuck in the storage space behind her seat.

_____

4. Maready eventually reached the shore, a grueling seven and a half hours after the crash.

_____

5. She went to the hospital, where she was admitted to intensive care.

_____

B. With a partner, discuss the parts of the sentences that you do understand.

Previewing will give you a general idea of what a text is about. To preview online articles, magazine articles, or academic texts:

1. Read the title and any subtitles.

2. Look at any photos, graphs, or charts.

3. Read the first sentence of each paragraph.

4. Read the last sentence of the text.

3 | Active Previewing

Preview the online article below. Underline the title, the first sentence of each paragraph, and the last sentence of the text as you preview. Then answer this question with a partner.

What do you think this text is about?

4 | Reading and Recalling

A. Read the text. Stop after each paragraph and tell a partner two things that you remember about it.

Survival at Sea

by Ronald Beermunder

> **REMEMBER**
> Skip the words and phrases that you do not understand.

1   It was November 1981, a dark, cold, moonless night off the South Carolina coast. After a day of scuba diving off Lady Island, Cathy Maready was tired and ready to go home. Instead of crossing the bridge and driving the 45 minutes home, she decided on a 15-minute Cessna flight. To save time, Maready decided not to file a flight plan. She took off from the uncontrolled local airport and headed home. No one knew that she was flying.

2   Three miles from the shore, the engine of the plane stopped. Maready tried to restart the engine, but she didn't succeed. She quickly prioritized[1] procedures that she learned in flight school: aviate, navigate, and communicate[2]. She began a slow descent and flawlessly landed the plane on the Atlantic Ocean.

continued

---

[1] **to prioritize:** to list or do things in order of importance

[2] **aviate, navigate, and communicate:** a phrase used by pilots to describe an emergency plan; literally, "fly, steer, and talk (on the radio)"

continued

3　She landed so smoothly and easily that the plane's emergency-locator transmitter (ELT) was not activated. The manual controls for the ELT were in the rear storage compartment of the plane. However, the cabin was slowly filling with water and fuel, and it was too dangerous to move to the back of the plane. Maready tried to retrieve her scuba gear, but the bag was stuck in the storage space behind her seat.

4　Less than 30 seconds later, Maready was treading water in the 59°F (15°C) Atlantic as she watched her airplane disappear into the ocean. The life expectancy for a person swimming in 59°F water is less than two hours. Then hypothermia[3] sets in, and eventually the body shuts down.

5　Maready started swimming west, using the stars to guide her toward shore. The weight of her wet clothes was too heavy, so she removed her shoes, her clothes, and even her watch. Maready knew that South Carolina recorded a very high number of shark attacks each year, and the thought frightened her. She kept swimming even though she was beginning to feel the effects of hypothermia. Maready couldn't stop thoughts of death from entering her mind, but she refused to give up the will to live.

6　As Maready swam, she began having hallucinations[4] of search boats, rescue helicopters, and sea monsters. She was exhausted, and she wanted to stop and yell for help, but she was afraid that she would drown. She decided that she wouldn't stop swimming until someone pulled her out of the frigid water, or until her feet touched the sand.

7　With strong determination[5], Maready eventually reached shore, a grueling seven and a half hours after the crash. As her mind was preparing her for death, her knees hit a sand bar, yet she was too numb to stand. With the shore so close, Maready was almost ready to cry from frustration. She swam around the sand bar out into deeper water, until she finally circled back and reached dry land. It was daybreak before she made it to the beach.

8　Maready was found staggering along the beach, suffering from shock and severe hypothermia. She went to the hospital, where she was admitted to intensive care. Doctors discovered that the chemicals in her body were so high from her physical effort that they couldn't even be measured. They were shocked that she was able to survive. Three days later, a healthy—and lucky—Maready was released from the hospital.

---

[3] **hypothermia:** abnormally low body temperature and a slowing down of all body functions
[4] **hallucination:** vision; dream
[5] **determination:** a strong purpose

B. Read the text again without pausing. Tell your partner two new things that you remember.

C. Work as a class or in large groups. Try to name as many things as you can about the text.

5 | Understanding the Text

A. Answer as many questions as you can without looking at the text. Discuss your answers with a partner.

1. Why did Maready decide to fly home?

   a. There was too much traffic on the road.

   b. She was tired and wanted to save time.

   c. There was an emergency at home, and she had to get back quickly.

2. What happened on the way home?

   a. She fell asleep.

   b. She had a car accident.

   c. The engine of her plane stopped.

3. How did Maready finally save herself?

   a. She swam to shore.

   b. A rescue boat picked her up.

   c. She walked home.

B. Write T for *True* and F for *False* according to the text. Discuss your answers with a partner.

   __F__ 1. Instead of flying home, Maready decided to drive.

   __F__ 2. Maready was able to restart the engine.

   __T__ 3. Maready landed the plane on the Atlantic Ocean.

   __F__ 4. Maready swam for two hours.

   __T__ 5. Maready spent three days in the hospital.

6 | Discussing the Issues

Answer the questions and discuss your answers with a partner.

1. Maready didn't tell anyone about her plans. Do you think she was careless? Why or why not?

2. Which strength do you think helped Maready more: her physical strength or her mental strength? Why?

3. What should you do before you leave on a trip alone?

Text 2 | A Difficult Choice

1 | Getting Started

A. Answer the questions and briefly discuss your answers with a partner.

1. Circle the letters of the activities you have done.

bike riding

rock climbing

hiking

2. Would you enjoy spending a Saturday afternoon doing any of these activities? Why or why not?

3. Name three things you should do before you leave on a day trip in nature.

B. Check (✔) the things that are useful to have on a one-day hiking trip. Briefly discuss your answers with a partner.

- ☐ 1. a blanket
- ☐ 2. a knife
- ☐ 3. a book
- ☑ 4. water
- ☐ 5. a mobile phone
- ☐ 6. a camera
- ☑ 7. food for the day
- ☑ 8. a sweater or jacket
- ☐ 9. an umbrella
- ☐ 10. a pen
- ☐ 11. candy
- ☐ 12. a hat

2 | Skipping Words and Phrases

A. Read the following sentences. First cross out the words and phrases you do not understand. Then write their parts of speech on the blanks.

1. He parked his truck and rode his bike fifteen miles to the Bluejohn Canyon Trailhead.
   (I understood all of it)

2. He couldn't move the massive boulder, so he tried to chip away at the rock with his knife.
   He couldn't move the massive _____, so he tried to _____ at the rock with his knife

3. By Tuesday, his food and water provisions were gone.
   By Tuesday, his food and water pro _____ were gone.

4. Next, Aron applied a tourniquet to his arm.
   Next, Aron applied _____ to his arm

5. The entire procedure took about one hour.
   The entire _____ took about one hour.

B. With a partner, discuss what you do understand about each sentence.

3 | Active Previewing

Preview the magazine article on the next page. Underline the title, the first sentence of each paragraph, and the last sentence of the text as you preview. Then answer this question with a partner.

What do you think this text is about? An accident by not telling his plans to anybody near or close to him.

4 | Reading and Recalling

A. Read the text. Stop after each paragraph and tell a partner two things that you remember about it.

The Only Way Out

BY SHANE BURROWS

1 On Saturday, April 26, 2003, Aron Ralston wanted to ride his bike and climb the rocks just outside the Canyonlands National Park in southeastern Utah. He parked his truck and rode his bike fifteen miles to the Bluejohn Canyon Trailhead.

2 Aron was wearing only a T-shirt and shorts when he started his hike. His backpack contained two burritos, less than a liter of water, a cheap knife, a small first-aid kit, a video camera, a digital camera, and rock-climbing gear. He did not have a jacket in his backpack.

3 When he reached Bluejohn Canyon, Aron tried to climb over the top of a large boulder. As Aron began to climb down the opposite side of the boulder, the 800-pound rock moved and trapped his right arm. He couldn't move the massive boulder, so he tried to chip away at the rock with his knife. It didn't work. He was stuck.

4 Temperatures dropped to near freezing that night, and still Aron worked to free himself. Sunday and Monday passed but he was still trapped. Sunlight reached the narrow canyon floor for only a very short period of time each day. By Tuesday, his food and water provisions were gone.

5 On Wednesday, Aron pulled out his video camera and recorded a message to his parents. He then scratched his name, birth date, and Wednesday's date into the canyon wall. He finished with *R.I.P.*[1]

6 On Thursday morning, however, after being trapped for five days, Aron had a vision. In Aron's mind, a small boy was running toward a one-armed man. Aron believed the boy was his future son and decided that he had to free himself. He knew that he had to do something drastic[2] now because he was quickly losing his strength.

> As Aron began to climb down the opposite side of the boulder, the 800-pound rock moved and trapped his right arm.

7 Aron realized he had to cut his arm off in order to survive. First, he forced his arm against the boulder to break it. Next, Aron applied a tourniquet to his arm, and used his knife to cut off his right arm below the elbow. The entire procedure took about one hour. Aron, with his arm in a self-made sling[3], then rappelled[4] nearly 70 feet down a rope to the bottom of Bluejohn Canyon, and hiked five miles into Horseshoe Canyon.

8 A Dutch family, in Utah on vacation, were hiking out of the canyon when they heard a voice cry, "Help, I need help!" They immediately realized that the voice must belong to the lost hiker they had heard about earlier in the day.

9 Aron walked toward the family and calmly told them he needed medical attention. The wife and son left the canyon immediately, in search of help. The husband and Aron followed at a slower speed.

continued

---

[1] **R.I.P.:** "Rest in Peace"; a common phrase that people put on tombstones

[2] **drastic:** severe; strong; serious

[3] **sling:** a piece of cloth used to support a broken arm

[4] **to rappel:** to go down the side of a rock or mountain on a rope

continued

10   In the meantime, Aron's friends began to worry when he didn't show up for work, and they called the authorities⁵. The problem was that Aron hadn't told anyone about his plans. Even his mother didn't know that her son was missing until Wednesday, when Aron's boss called her. A search party was quickly formed, and a helicopter was soon in the air.

11   On Thursday, the helicopter crew saw a group of people waving at them from the canyon floor. The crew landed the helicopter in a wide space near the canyon and stared at the group of people in amazement. Aron was walking toward them, weak but alive. Aron Ralston had rescued himself.

---

⁵ **the authorities:** people legally responsible for public safety, such as the police, the fire department, or mountain search and rescue teams

B. Read the text again without pausing. Tell your partner two new things that you remember.

C. Work as a class or in large groups. Try to name as many things as you can about the text.

5 | Understanding the Text

A. Answer as many questions as you can without looking at the text. Discuss your answers with a partner.

1. Why did Aron go to Bluejohn Canyon?

   a. to work

   b. to ride his bike and climb the rocks

   c. to look for a lost friend

2. What happened to Aron in the canyon?

   a. He got lost.

   b. He fell in a river.

   c. His arm was trapped by a rock.

3. What did Aron finally do?

   a. He fell asleep.

   b. He cut off his arm.

   c. He waited for his friends to find him.

B. Check (✔) the events that occurred according to the text.

   ☑ 1. Aron ran out of food and water.

   ☐ 2. Aron went hiking with friends.

   ☐ 3. Aron was bitten by a snake.

   ☑ 4. Aron recorded a video message to his parents.

   ☑ 5. Aron's friends worried when he didn't show up for work.

☑ 6. Aron met a Dutch family.

☑ 7. A helicopter came to get Aron.

☐ 8. Aron's mother came to rescue him.

6 | Discussing the Issues

Answer the questions and discuss your answers with a partner.

1. Do you think people should tell someone where they are going when they go into nature by themselves? Why or why not?

2. Do you think you could do what Aron did? Why or why not?

3. What lesson(s) do you think we can learn from Aron's experience?

Text 3 | To the Rescue

1 | Getting Started

Answer the questions and briefly discuss your answers with a partner.

1. Have you ever been lost?

2. When you were little, did anyone give you advice about what to do if you got lost?

3. Who helps people who get lost, stranded, or injured in the mountains?

> **GRAPHICS** Previewing Graphs and Charts
>
> **Graphs and charts** give a picture of statistical information. **Preview** graphs by reading the title, any introductory information, the *x*-axis (←→) and *y*-axis (↑↓) titles, and any **boldfaced** or *italicized* information.

2 | Active Previewing

Preview the graph on the next page and then answer the questions. Discuss your answers with a partner.

1. What is the title of the graph? _North Shore Rescue_

2. What are the axis titles?

   a. *x*-axis (the horizontal ←→ axis) _Year_

   b. *y*-axis (the vertical ↑↓ axis) _Number of emergency call response._

3. What is the subject of this graph? _~~North Shore Rescue~~ Increasing_

North Shore Rescue

North Shore Rescue (NSR) provides free life-saving mountain search and rescue services. The team has helped rescue many stranded or injured hikers, climbers, skiers, snowboarders, and mountain bikers.

The graph below shows the number of emergency calls that NSR has responded to for the years 1992 through 2005.

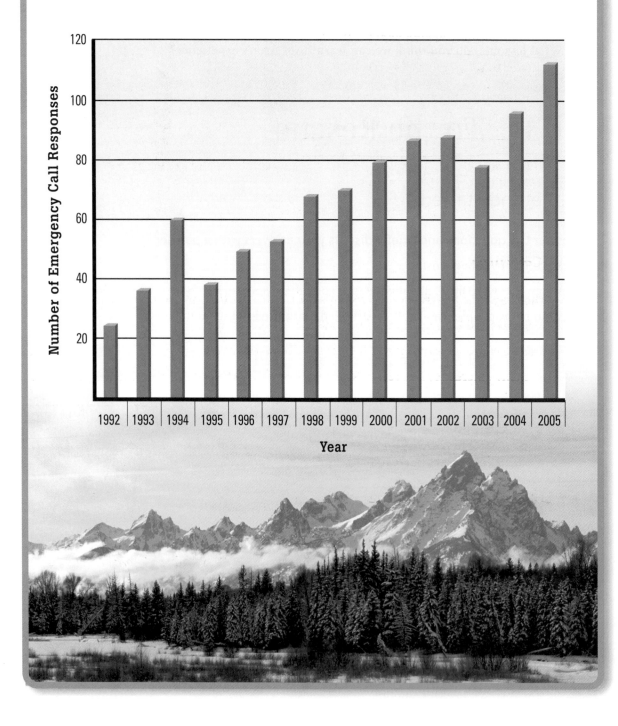

Scanning is looking for information quickly before or after you read a text. You can scan for numbers, symbols, bolded items, names, key words, or brief answers to questions. To scan:

1. Decide on what you want to find: a date, the name of a company, or the number of teens who use the Internet, for example.

2. Predict what you will be looking for: capital letters, numbers, or symbols, for instance.

3. Move your eyes quickly across the page—with the help of your finger or a pencil, if you want—looking only for the item you want to find.

Refer to the graph to answer the following question.

How many emergency call responses were there in 1994?

In order to find the answer, first we scan the *Year* axis (←→) and find *1994*. Then we follow up to the top of the bar and look over at the *Number of Emergency Call Responses* axis (↑↓) to find the answer. You do not need to read the other information. The answer is *60*.

3 | Scanning

Scan the graph for the answers to the questions. Discuss your answers with a partner.

1. Which year had the most emergency call responses? _2005_

2. Which year had approximately 70 emergency call responses? _1999_

3. How many emergency call responses were there in 2000? _80_

4. Which year had fewer emergency call responses: 2002 or 2003? _2003_

5. In general, has there been an increase or a decrease in the number of emergency call responses? _An increase._

4 | Discussing the Issues

Answer the questions and discuss your answers with a partner.

1. Why do you think there might have been an increase in the number of emergency calls over the last 10 years?

2. Would you like to be part of an emergency rescue team? Why or why not?

3. How do you think it is possible for North Shore Rescue to offer its services for free?

Text 4 | Antarctic Survivors

1 | Getting Started

A. Answer the questions and briefly discuss your answers with a partner.

1. Do you like to be outdoors in cold weather?

2. Where do you think the ship in the photograph is?

  (a). Antarctica

  b. Britain

  c. South America

3. Match the outdoor health dangers with their definitions on the right.

  ___b___ **1.** frostbite   a. extreme physical tiredness

  ___c___ **2.** malnutrition   b. injury to the skin from overexposure to freezing temperatures

  ___a___ **3.** exhaustion   c. a state caused by not enough food or not enough variety of food

B. Answer the questions and briefly discuss your answers with a partner.

1. Check (✔) all of the qualities that make a good leader on an outdoor trip.

A good leader should ...	
✔ a. ... be courageous or brave.	✔ e. ... be a good listener.
☐ b. ... be optimistic and cheerful.	✔ f. ... keep the team safe.
☐ c. ... have common sense.	☐ g. ... be a good cook.
✔ d. ... have good organization skills.	☐ h. ... have a good sense of humor.

2. Write the top three qualities from your choices in question *1*.

Be courageous or brave.

Keep the team safe.

Be a good listener.

3. Write one more quality that is important in a leader.

Be fair.

2 | Skipping Words and Phrases

A. Read the following sentences. First cross out the words and phrases you do not understand. Then write their parts of speech on the blanks.

1. In 1914, Sir Ernest Shackleton led an <u>expedition</u> to the Antarctic.

   _____

2. It was near the beginning of the Antarctic summer, but just two days later the ship met <u>pack ice.</u>

   _____

3. Caroline Alexander, author of *The <u>Endurance,</u>* describes Shackleton as "a leader who put his men first."

   _____

4. They were separated from the <u>whaling station</u> by 22 miles of mountainous <u>terrain.</u>

   _____

5. The <u>marooned</u> men went crazy with excitement when they saw the little boat <u>approach</u> with Shackleton himself aboard.

   _____

B. With a partner, discuss what you do understand about each sentence.

3 | Active Previewing

A. Preview the academic text on the next page. Underline the title, the first sentence of each paragraph, and the last sentence of the text as you preview. Then tell a partner two things you remember about it.

> **REMEMBER**
> Preview longer academic texts a second time.

B. Answer this question with a partner.

What is this text about?

4 | Reading and Recalling

A. Read the text. Stop after each paragraph and tell a partner two things that you remember about it.

Walking Out of History—The True Story of Shackleton's Endurance[1] Expedition[2]

by John Rabe

1   In 1914, Sir Ernest Shackleton led an expedition to the Antarctic. Today, this famous trip still excites a new generation of adventurers. And they especially admire Shackleton because he showed such strong leadership and courage during extreme difficulties.

2   Shackleton's plan was to cross the continent of Antarctica on foot. In his words, the Imperial Trans-Antarctic Expedition of 1914 was to be "a wonderful journey." And it was, though not in the way he imagined. He and his crew of 27 men were trapped in Antarctica for almost two years, fighting ice, the ocean, and temperatures that sometimes dropped to -30°C (-22°F). The world gave them up for dead.

3   The *Endurance* left South Georgia Island, approximately 1,600 kilometers east of the southern tip of South America, on December 5, 1914. It was near the beginning of the Antarctic summer, but just two days later the ship met pack ice. At this time of year, the pack ice was farther north than anyone could remember. At first the ship was able to break through the ice, but on January 18, 1915, it became trapped for good.

4   The men waited patiently while hoping that the ship would be released. Shackleton organized soccer and hockey games or competitions in order to keep the men's spirits high during the wait. Again and again they tried to free the *Endurance*. Sometimes they would follow a narrow crack that appeared in the ice. Other times they tried to chop their way through the thick ice to get to open water. None of these efforts succeeded, however.

5   In the end, the ship was crushed by the pressure of the ice. As the men moved the supplies and their dogs from the boat to the surface of the ice, they could hear the sound of the ship breaking apart. They saved food and tools and three lifeboats. They watched as the *Endurance* gradually sank down into the depths of the Antarctic sea.

REMEMBER
Skip the words and phrases that you do not understand.

6   It was October 27, 1915, and the *Endurance* crew was marooned[3] 560 kilometers from land in subzero cold. Shackleton knew that being trapped in these extreme conditions could make his men go crazy, but he decided not to let that happen. He was also determined that no lives would be lost. Caroline Alexander, author of *The Endurance*, describes Shackleton as "a leader who put his men first." His crew called him "The Boss" and believed he had the power to save them from disaster[4].

7   The crew had to make camp on the ice and wait nearly six months for the ice to break up. When it happened, the ice floe that they were on broke in two, and they were separated from the lifeboats. Luckily, they managed to get the boats back. Shackleton ordered the men into the boats, and they set out for Elephant Island, 160 kilometers away.

8   It was a fierce, seven-day journey to Elephant Island in the open boats. The men passed a week of wet, cold, hunger, and thirst. They avoided huge pieces of floating ice and endured impossibly rough seas. At last they reached land—the first solid ground they'd stood on in 497 days. The group was in bad shape, suffering from frostbite, malnutrition, and exhaustion.

9   Shackleton knew that no one would come to search for them on Elephant Island, and they could not survive there for long. He decided that their only hope was to get to the whaling station

continued

---

[1] *Endurance*/**endurance:** 1) the name of the ship Shackleton took to the Antarctic; 2) perseverance; the ability to withstand stress or difficulties

[2] **expedition:** a trip that is made by many people with a specific goal

[3] **to be marooned:** to be stuck without help in a situation far from civilization

[4] **disaster:** an event that is very bad; a severe misfortune

continued

on South Georgia Island, nearly 1100 kilometers to the east. He chose five of his strongest men—including the captain of the *Endurance*, who was to be the navigator—to join him on this dangerous journey. They climbed into a seven-meter lifeboat and set off.

10   A ship's navigator, or guide, is responsible for calculating the ship's position on the water. He uses a sextant to make the calculations, and it is difficult to get an accurate reading even in good weather conditions. On the journey to the whaling station, Shackleton's navigator was only able to take four unreliable readings of the sun. They were not sure, therefore, if they would even reach their goal. But, amazingly, they did, after 17 days at sea.

11   Bad weather caused the group to land on the wrong side of the island. They were separated from the whaling station by 22 miles of moun-tainous terrain. Three of the men could not make the trek[5], so Shackleton and two others crossed the glacier-covered mountains. They made their entry into the whaling station through a waterfall.

12   Four months passed before Shackleton was able to rescue the men on Elephant Island. He tried three times, but the winter ice prevented the different boats from reaching the island. He finally succeeded in a small Chilean tugboat called the *Yelcho*.

13   The marooned men went crazy with excitement when they saw the little boat approach with Shackleton himself aboard. They had all survived 105 lonely days on Elephant Island, waiting for Shackleton to return. When the boat neared, Shackleton stood up in its bow, calling, "Are you all well?" The men answered, "All safe, Boss, all well."

---

[5] **trek:** a slow and/or difficult journey, especially on foot

B. Read the text again without pausing. Tell your partner two new things that you remember.

C. Work as a class or in large groups. Try to name as many things as you can about the text.

5 | Understanding the Text

A. Answer as many questions as you can without looking at the text. Discuss your answers with a partner.

1. Who was the leader of the *Endurance* expedition?

     a. Caroline Alexander

     b. Ernest Shackleton

     c. the captain of the *Endurance*

2. Why couldn't Shackleton and his men cross Antarctica as they had planned?

     a. The British navy required the ship for the World War I naval effort.

     b. Their ship, the *Endurance,* became trapped in the ice as it approached Antarctica.

     c. The winter conditions were so bad that they had to turn around and go back to Britain.

3. What finally happened to the *Endurance*?

   a. It broke apart from the pressure of the ice and sank.

   b. It was trapped in the ice and the men had to leave it where it was.

   c. It crashed into the rocks near Elephant Island and sank.

4. How did the men reach Elephant Island?

   a. by walking over icy land

   b. on a Chilean tugboat

   c. in three lifeboats from the *Endurance*

5. Who rescued the remaining men on Elephant Island?

   a. Ernest Shackleton

   b. the British navy

   c. Norwegian fishermen

B. Complete the sentences according to the text.

1. Today, Ernest Shackleton is still admired for his _____.

   a. navigation skills

   b. strong leadership

   c. sports abilities

2. Shackleton _____.

   a. was the first explorer to cross Antarctica on foot

   b. went to hunt whales in Antarctica

   c. was not able to cross Antarctica on foot

3. During the expedition, _____ men died.

   a. no

   b. two

   c. three

6 | Discussing the Issues

Answer the questions and discuss your answers with a partner.

1. Was Shackleton a good leader? Why or why not?

2. If you had a chance to explore Antarctica, would you go? Why or why not?

3. Why do you think many explorers are willing to live in difficult and terrible conditions while they are away on their trips?

Putting It On Paper

A. Write a one-paragraph letter on one of these topics.

1. Your friend is going alone on a one-week hiking trip in the mountains and needs advice.

2. Your friend is going to learn to fly an airplane for personal trips and pleasure and needs advice.

Steps for your letter

a. State your opinion about your friend's trip in the first sentence; this is your thesis statement or topic sentence.

b. Give your friend three specific pieces of advice about what he or she should do and prepare before leaving that relate to your opinion.

c. Summarize your ideas in a final sentence, wish your friend well, and close your letter.

B. Exchange letters with a partner. First read your partner's letter and answer the questions in the checklist. Then give feedback to your partner.

✔ CHECKLIST
1. Is your partner's opinion stated in the first sentence?
2. Are there three specific pieces of advice to support the first sentence?
3. Are you persuaded by your partner's advice?
4. Is any of the information not related to the topic? If yes, please underline it on your partner's paper and then write it below:

_____

_____

_____

_____

_____

_____

_____

C. Revise your letter based on your partner's feedback.

Taking It Online | Exploring the Unknown

A. With a partner, use the Internet to research one female explorer and one male explorer.

1. Use Google (www.google.com) or another major search engine to begin your online research.

2. Search for information about one female and one male explorer. Here are some examples to get you started:

Hannu	Amelia Earhart	Gudridur Thorbjarnardottir
Zhang Qian	Ferdinand Magellan	Yuri Gagarin
Isabelle Eberhardt	Sue Hendrickson	Sacagawea
Leif Eriksson	Abu Abdullah Muhammad	Ibn Battuta

3. Preview the websites as you would a magazine article or an essay.

B. Complete the tables with the information you find.

Explorer:	Ernest Shackleton	
Website address:	americanradioworks.publicradio.org	☑ Man ☐ Woman
When he or she explored:	early 1900s	
Where he or she explored:	Antarctica	
One interesting fact:	saved all of his men after they were lost for two years in Antarctica	

Explorer:		
Website address:		☐ Man ☐ Woman
When he or she explored:		
Where he or she explored:		
One interesting fact:		

Explorer:		
Website address:		☐ Man ☐ Woman
When he or she explored:		
Where he or she explored:		
One interesting fact:		

C. Following up. Tell your classmates the facts you discovered. See if they can guess which explorer you researched.

Chapter 2

The Musical Mind

Answer the questions and briefly discuss your answers with a partner.

1. Do you play a musical instrument, or do you know anyone who does?

2. Look at the photos. What is each person doing?

3. What are some reasons why people play musical instruments or compose music?

Text 1 | Feel the Beat

1 | Getting Started

A. Which instruments can you name? Match the photos with the instrument names.

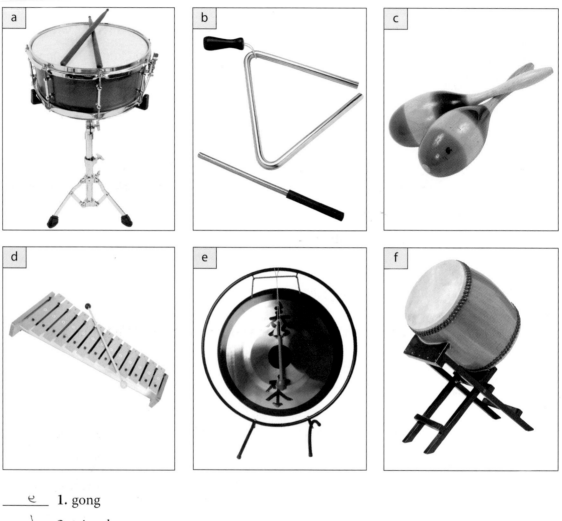

| a | b | c |
| d | e | f |

_____e_____ **1.** gong

_____b_____ **2.** triangle

_____c_____ **3.** maracas

_____a_____ **4.** snare drum

_____f._____ **5.** Taiko drum

_____d_____ **6.** xylophone

B. Answer the questions and briefly discuss your answers with a partner.

1. Have you ever played or heard any of the percussion instruments in the photos?

2. Check (✔) all the senses that are important for playing percussion instruments.

☐ a. hearing   ☐ d. taste

☐ b. sight   ☐ e. touch

☐ c. smell

C. Check (✔) all of the activities that might be difficult to do with a loss of hearing.

☐ 1. going shopping   ☐ 5. playing sports

☐ 2. listening to music   ☐ 6. talking on a mobile phone

☐ 3. painting and drawing   ☐ 7. watching television

☐ 4. playing a musical instrument   ☐ 8. writing music

2 | Active Previewing

Preview the magazine article below. Underline the title, the first sentence of each paragraph, and the last sentence of the text as you preview. Then answer the questions with a partner.

1. Who is this text about? _Evelyn Glennie._

2. What do you think this text is about? _percussionist._

3 | Reading and Recalling

A. Read the text. Stop after each paragraph and tell a partner two things that you remember about it.

Evelyn Glennie, Solo Percussionist

BY SILVER BURDETT

1   Evelyn Glennie, a percussionist[1], began to lose her hearing when she was eight years old. By the time she was twelve, she was profoundly deaf[2]. Born in 1965, she grew up on a farm in northeast Scotland, where her mother was the organist[3] in the village church. Under her mother's musical influence, Evelyn played harmonica and clarinet as a child.

2   Around the same time she lost her hearing, Evelyn discovered the snare drum and decided to become a professional percussionist. She attended the Royal College of Music in London, where she found out that there had never before been anyone who made a living[4] as a solo percussionist. But it was too late to stop her—she was sure that being a percussionist was

> **REMEMBER**
> Skip the words and phrases you do not understand.

continued

---

[1] **percussionist:** a person who plays percussion instruments, such as drums, bells, gongs, and rattles

[2] **profoundly deaf:** able to hear some sounds, but cannot understand words by sounds alone

[3] **organist:** a person who plays an organ (a keyboard instrument similar to a piano, but with a different sound)

[4] **to make a living:** to earn enough money to pay for one's expenses (such as housing, food, and clothing)

continued

what she wanted to do with her life.

3   Glennie can hear sounds and can tell them apart even though she cannot hear them the way she did long ago. For example, she can hear that someone is speaking, but cannot hear words clearly, so she reads lips to get the meaning. Or when she hears a kind of crackling sound, Evelyn knows that the crackling sound is a phone ringing.

4   Glennie has become a successful musician with a very busy schedule. In 1989, her first recording won a Grammy award. Since then, she has made twelve more recordings and has appeared on television. Glennie is the world's first full-time solo percussionist, and she has performed on five different continents and in about 40 different countries. She often performs as a soloist with symphony orchestras, and she performs about 110 concerts each year. And even with her busy schedule, Glennie finds time for her hobbies; she loves painting, drawing, and exploring antique stores. She has not let deafness stand in her way.

5   Glennie owns about 1,400 percussion instruments. While most people travel with one or two suitcases, Glennie travels with up to two tons (about 2,000 kilograms) of percussion equipment. It takes about four hours to set up her instruments for each concert and two hours to take them down again.

6   Glennie is not just a performer, though. She also designs and sells her own percussion instruments from unusual materials. Some of the materials she uses to make these instruments include sheet metal and scaffolding[5]. And because of Glennie's interest in making unique instruments, a composer named Django Bates wrote a musical piece for her named "My Dream Kitchen." All of the musical instruments used in this piece are kitchen tools!

7   Evelyn Glennie wants people to focus on her music rather than on her hearing loss, and she wants them to be entertained. She explains that being deaf is poorly understood by most people. And in her case, it didn't prevent her from doing what she wanted to do.

---

[5] **scaffolding:** a temporary frame (made of wood or metal) that is built next to a wall and supports the people who are building or repairing the wall

B. Read the text again without pausing. Tell your partner two new things that you remember.

C. Work as a class or in large groups. Try to name as many things as you can about the text.

4 | Understanding the Text

A. Answer as many questions as you can without looking at the text. Discuss your answers with a partner.

1. Who is Evelyn Glennie?

   a. a music instructor

   c. a percussionist

   b. an organist

2. What happened to Glennie when she was a child?

   a. Django Bates wrote a musical piece for her.

   b. She began to lose her hearing.

   c. She won a Grammy award.

3. What does Glennie design and sell?

   a. her paintings

   b. percussion instruments

   c. kitchen tools

B. Which photo best illustrates the kind of instruments Evelyn Glennie plays? Circle your answer.

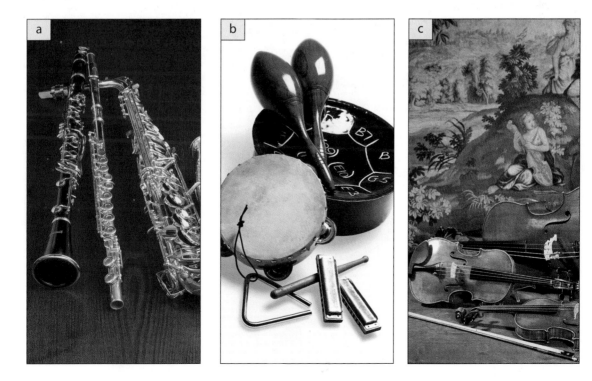

a

b

c

The **topic** of a list is the subject of the list. The topic is always expressed as a word or a phrase (not a complete sentence). When identifying the topic of a list, choose the word or phrase that best describes all of the elements of the list.

Read the list of possible topics.

harmonicas

organs

clarinets

musical instruments

snare drums

Harmonicas, organs, clarinets, and snare drums are all examples of *musical instruments*. The best topic for this list is *musical instruments*.

5 | Understanding the Topic—Lists

Read the lists and circle the item that is the topic.

1. painting

hobbies

drawing

exploring antique stores

2. winning a Grammy award

important moments in Glennie's life

losing her hearing when she was eight

becoming the world's first solo percussionist

3. percussionist

instrument maker

Evelyn Glennie

soloist

The **topic** is the subject of a text or a paragraph. The topic is always expressed as a word or a phrase (not a complete sentence). To identify the topic:

1. Choose a word or phrase that most clearly describes the subject of the whole paragraph or text.

2. Do not choose a topic that is too general.

3. Do not choose a topic that is too specific.

Reread ¶1 on page 23. The possible choices for the topic are:

    a. Evelyn Glennie's life

    b. Evelyn Glennie's mother

    c. Evelyn Glennie's childhood

Choice *a* is too general. This paragraph only discusses a part of her life.

Choice *b* is too specific. It is only one detail of the paragraph.

Choice *c* is the best topic for ¶1.

6 | Understanding the Topic—Text and Paragraphs

A. Text. Write *T* for *Topic*, *G* for *Too General*, and *S* for *Too Specific*. Discuss your answers with a partner.

1. What is the topic of the text?

    a. ___S___ Evelyn Glennie's musical instruments

    b. ___G___ percussionists

    c. ___T___ Evelyn Glennie

2. Is your answer for the topic here the same as the one you determined after you previewed the text, or is your answer different? _____

B. Paragraphs. Write *T* for *Topic*, *G* for *Too General*, and *S* for *Too Specific*. Discuss your answers with a partner.

1. What is the topic of ¶3?

    a. ___T___ how Glennie hears

    b. ___G___ sounds

    c. ___S___ how a ringing phone sounds to Glennie

2. What is the topic of ¶4?

    a. ___S___ Glennie's hobbies

    b. ___G___ a successful musician

    c. ___T___ Glennie's busy schedule

3. What is the topic of ¶5?

a. ___S___ how long it takes to set up Glennie's instruments

b. ___G___ percussion equipment

c. ___T___ Glennie's percussion instruments

VOCAB **VOCABULARY STRATEGY** Understanding Subject and Object Pronouns

Pronouns refer to nouns. We use pronouns to avoid repeating the same nouns over and over again. Usually, a pronoun refers to the closest and/or most logical noun (or pronoun) that comes before it in the sentence or paragraph.

A **subject pronoun** replaces a noun as the subject of a sentence or clause. The subject pronouns are **I, you, he, she, it, we, you,** and **they.**

Read the following examples.

1. Glennie can hear sounds and can tell them apart even though *she* cannot hear them the way she did long ago. (¶3)

Glennie is not the closest noun that comes before *she* in the sentence, but it is the most logical. *She* refers to Glennie.

Note: When a pronoun is in a dependant clause, it often refers to the noun that appears after it.

2. Around the same time *she* lost her hearing, Evelyn discovered the snare drum. (¶2)

She refers to Evelyn.

Note: Sometimes *it* does not refer to a noun in the text, but is used as the subject of a sentence stating a general truth or fact: *It's really hot out today,* or *It is enjoyable to play music.* We call this use "it insertion."

3. But *it* was too late to stop her—she was sure that being a percussionist was what she wanted to do with her life. (¶2)

It does not refer to a noun in the text.

An **object pronoun** replaces a noun as the object of a sentence, clause, or phrase. The object pronouns are **me, you, him, her, it, us, you,** and **them.**

Read the following example.

Glennie can hear sounds and can tell *them* apart even though she cannot hear them the way she did long ago. (¶3)

Sounds is the closest and the most logical noun that comes before *them* in the sentence. *Them* refers to *sounds*.

7 | Understanding Subject and Object Pronouns

Write the subject or object that the pronoun refers to according to the text. Discuss your answers with a partner.

1. she (when she was eight) (¶1) _Evelyn Glennie_

2. them (cannot hear them) (¶3) _Sounds_

3. she (when she hears a crackling sound) (¶3) _____

4. them (take them down) (¶5) _Instrument._

5. it (it didn't prevent her) (¶7) _____

8 | Discussing the Issues

Answer the questions and discuss your answers with a partner.

1. What are some of the advantages and disadvantages of being a famous musician?

2. Is it surprising that a deaf woman is a successful percussionist? Why or why not?

3. Why do you think there are not more solo percussionists?

Text 2 | Wild Music

1 | Getting Started

A. Match the words below with the photos and discuss your answers with a partner.

_b_ 1. upright piano

_c_ 2. symphony orchestra

_a_ 3. grand piano

B. Answer the questions and briefly discuss your answers with a partner.

1. Which instrument above (*a* or *b*) would you find in a symphony orchestra?

2. Do you think a wolf would make a good pet? Why or why not?

C. Check (✔) the qualities necessary for a professional musician. Briefly discuss your answers with a partner.

Professional musicians should have...	Necessary	Not necessary
1. ... patience.	☐	☐
2. ... energy and passion.	☐	☐
3. ... mental strength.	☐	☐
4. ... concentration.	☐	☐
5. ... physical strength.	☐	☐

2 | Active Previewing

Preview the online article on the next page. Underline the title, the first sentence of each paragraph, and the last sentence of the text as you preview. Then answer the questions with a partner.

1. Who is this text about? *Helen Grimaud*

2. What do you think this text is about?

A. Read the text. Stop after each paragraph and tell a partner two things that you remember about it.

Leader of the Pack

by Heidi Waleson

REMEMBER
Skip the words and phrases that you do not understand.

1   Pianist Hélène Grimaud has two passions[1]: music and wolves. She lives in a small house an hour's drive outside New York City. It is convenient to area airports, and Grimaud often travels to play piano with ensembles[2] such as the Los Angeles Philharmonic and the Orchestre de Paris. Grimaud's property also has enough space for her three British Columbian wolves, which she raised herself.

2   Grimaud is petite, or small, in size, but she has a strong and passionate character. She calls herself a "control freak": she edits her own recordings, makes her own travel arrangements, and limits her concert engagements to ten days a month. She doesn't like to be away from her wolves for longer than that. Her intense energy explodes in performances of stunning beauty and depth that dazzle (amaze) her audiences. This energy also fuels—supports—her passion for wolves, creatures that she believes have been treated unfairly in literature and history.

3   The wolves—Apache, Lucas, and Kayla—live in a two-acre enclosure, a yard surrounded by a high double fence. When Grimaud visits them, she wears padded overalls[3]. Apache, a big white two-year-old male and leader of the pack, joyously greets Grimaud and is almost doglike in his delight. The other two wolves are more reserved, or shy. "Wolves are like most wild creatures," Grimaud says. "They want to be left alone."

4   The pianist's first encounter[4] with wolves was in Florida with a female wolf-dog hybrid. Grimaud recalls that the animal was afraid of everything. "She wasn't even comfortable with her owner," says Grimaud. But the animal was comfortable with Grimaud, who was the only person who could get close to her. Grimaud was interested in how the wolf-dog hybrid's behavior was so different from dogs' behavior. The attraction Grimaud felt for the wolves was immediate.

continued

---

[1] **passion:** strong emotion or interest in something or someone
[2] **ensemble:** here, a musical group
[3] **overalls:** protective clothing worn over regular clothing
[4] **encounter:** meeting, especially an unexpected or brief one

continued

5   Grimaud's attraction to the piano was immediate, too. While growing up in Aix-en-Provence, France, she was a difficult child. Her teachers found that she asked inappropriate[5] questions in class. And she always finished her schoolwork first and then bothered the other students. Furthermore, she was a loner—a person who prefers to be alone. Her parents tried to get her interested in sports, martial arts, and dance, but nothing interested her—until music.

6   Grimaud believes that music appealed to, or attracted, her because she had so much imagination. "Real life wasn't good enough … It was obviously in my head. Music was mentally captivating." Grimaud progressed fast. She began studying at the Paris Conservatory at 13, played her first concerto concert at 14, and made her first recording a year later. She also finished her high-school studies and completed a bachelor's degree in ethology (the study of animal behavior) by correspondence.

7   Grimaud spends all of the money she earns from her concerts on her wolves. Therefore, the small living room of her Westchester home contains a simple black Yamaha upright piano instead of an expensive grand piano. Grimaud does most of her practicing in her head, anyway, a method that avoids unnecessary injury or strain to her hands. Practicing music mentally also makes her playing sound more fresh in concert.

8   Grimaud's mental strength is also an advantage when she is with her wolves, which require complete attention when she is in their enclosure. She believes that it is safer to show the wolves that she is their equal rather than their superior, and that requires constant attention. "Once you enter their world as a member of the group, even a part-time member, you expose yourself to being challenged," she says, explaining that wolves like to have the advantage.

9   That contact with the wolves, Grimaud says, is inspiring and educational. "There's something very musical in it," she says. "The quality of concentration you need … to interact with a wild animal … [is] identical to what you need with a piece of music." In both cases, she explains, you must interact with a creature—a wolf or music—that is completely different from you.

---

[5] **inappropriate:** not suitable or proper

B. Read the text again without pausing. Tell your partner two new things that you remember.

C. Work as a class or in large groups. Try to name as many things as you can about the text.

4 | Understanding the Text

A. Answer as many questions as you can without looking at the text. Discuss your answers with a partner.

1. What is Hélène Grimaud's profession? _Pianist_

2. Aside from her profession, what is Hélène's other passion? _Wolves._

3. Check (✔) the adjectives that best describe Hélène Grimaud:

   ☑ a. passionate and unusual

   ☐ b. funny and friendly

   ☐ c. quiet and honest

B. Complete the sentences according to the text.

_d_	1. Grimaud's wolves are from	a. Paris, France.
_c_	2. Hélène Grimaud first encountered a wolf-dog hybrid in	b. Aix-en-Provence, France.
_b_	3. Hélène grew up in	c. Florida.
_a_	4. Grimaud studied at the conservatory in	d. British Columbia.
_e_	5. Grimaud lives in	e. Westchester, New York.

5 | Understanding the Topic

A. Lists. Read the lists and circle the item that is the topic.

1. New York

   Los Angeles

   cities

   Paris

2. intense

   qualities

   energetic

   passionate

3. dance

   interests

   martial arts

   music

B. Text. Write *T* for *Topic*, *G* for *Too General*, and *S* for *Too Specific*. Discuss your answers with a partner.

1. What is the topic of the text?

    a. __S__ Hélène Grimaud's passion for wolves

    b. __T__ Hélène Grimaud, a pianist who raises wolves

    c. __G__ classical music and wolves

2. Is your answer for the topic here the same as the one you determined after you previewed the text, or is your answer different? _____

C. Paragraphs. Write *T* for *Topic*, *G* for *Too General*, and *S* for *Too Specific*. Discuss your answers with a partner.

1. What is the topic of ¶1?

    a. __G__ music and wolves

    b. __T__ Hélène Grimaud's two passions

    c. __S__ Hélène Grimaud's three British Columbian wolves

2. What is the topic of ¶3?

    a. __T__ Grimaud's wolves

    b. __G__ wolves

    c. __S__ Apache, Grimaud's two-year-old male wolf

3. What is the topic of ¶4?

    a. __T__ Hélène's first encounter with wolves

    b. __S__ the wolf-dog hybrid's fear

    c. __G__ wolves in Florida

4. What is the topic of ¶6?

    a. __S~~T~~__ Grimaud's first concerto

    b. __G__ music and imagination

    c. __T~~S~~__ Grimaud's attraction to music

5. What is the topic of ¶9?

    a. __S~~*~~__ concentration with wolves

    b. __T~~S~~__ the concentration required to interact with wolves and music

    c. __G__ concentration

One strategy for understanding unfamiliar words is to look for **synonyms**. Synonyms are words that have the same or a similar meaning. Synonyms of potentially unfamiliar words are often set apart from the main sentence by commas (,), dashes (—), or parentheses (( )).

Read the following sentences.

1. Grimaud is *petite*, or small, in size. (¶2)

   What is *petite*? The comma + *or* (, or) indicate that *petite* means *small*.

2. This energy also *fuels*—supports—her passion for wolves. (¶2)

   What does *fuels* mean? The dashes (—) indicate that *fuels* means *supports*.

3. She also ... completed a bachelor's degree in *ethology* (the study of animal behavior). (¶6)

   What is *ethology*? The parentheses (( )) show that *ethology* means *the study of animal behavior*.

6 | Understanding Vocabulary in Context—Synonyms

Write the best synonym for each word or phrase according to the text.

1. to dazzle (¶2) _to amaze_
2. enclosure (¶3) _to surround_
3. reserved (¶3) _shy_
4. loner (¶5) _a person who prefers to be alone._
5. to appeal to (¶6) _attracted_

7 | Discussing the Issues

Answer the questions and discuss your answers with a partner.

1. Why do you think the wolves feel comfortable with Hélène Grimaud?

2. Do you think it is a good idea to raise and keep an animal that normally lives in the wild? Why or why not?

3. How can pursuing a passion—like music—help someone in life?

Text 3 | The Classical Advantage

1 | Getting Started

Answer the questions and briefly discuss your answers with a partner.

1. Have you ever listened to music while studying?

2. Do you think listening to music can improve a student's scores in some subjects? Explain.

3. Complete the table. In your opinion, how could listening to classical music while studying affect a student's performance in class?

Listening to classical music while studying ...	... could improve my scores.	... could lower my scores.	... would have no affect on my scores.
a. math	☐	☐	☑
b. writing	☑	☐	☐
c. reading	☐	☑	☐

2 | Active Previewing

REMEMBER

Preview graphs by reading the title, the introductory information, and the x-axis and y-axis titles. For more on *previewing graphs*, see page 11.

Preview the bar graph below and then answer the questions.

1. What is the title of the bar graph? *Listening to Classical Music*

2. What are the titles of the x-axis and y-axis? *x → Subject. y → Percentage correct*

3. What is the topic of this bar graph? *Will music effect on their study?*

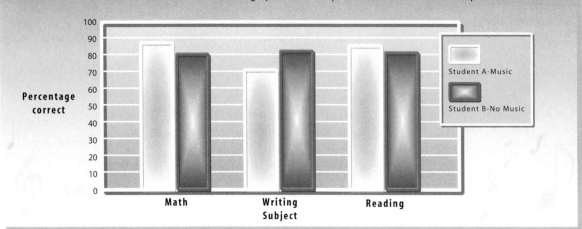

Listening to Classical Music Affects Two Students' Academic Performance

Two students practiced their math, writing, and reading skills. *Student A* listened to classical music during the practice activities. *Student B* did not listen to music. The bar graph below compares the students' academic performance.

3 | Scanning

Scan the bar graph for the answers to the questions. Discuss your answers with a partner.

1. Which student listened to music while studying (Student A or Student B)?
   Student A

2. What kind of music did this student listen to? _classical_

3. Which student got a higher percentage in math? _A_

4. In which subject did Student A get about 72 percent? _Writing_

5. In which subject did Student B score higher than Student A? _Writing_

4 | Discussing the Issues

Answer the questions and discuss your answers with a partner.

1. The bar graph compares the academic performance of only two students. Aside from listening to classical music, what other factors might have affected these students' performances?

2. If studies show that listening to classical music can be helpful with some subjects, do you think that teachers should play this music in the classroom? Why or why not?

3. The bar graph shows the effect of classical music on academic performance. How do you think the results might be different (if at all) if the students were listening to different music, such as techno, pop, rap, or rock? Why?

Text 4 | A Musical Mystery Solved

1 | Getting Started

A. Answer the questions and briefly discuss your answers with a partner.

1. Do you like classical music? Why or why not? _Depends on what music._

2. Check (✔) all the Western classical composers that you have heard of (if any).

   - ☑ a. Johann Sebastian Bach
   - ☑ b. Antonio Vivaldi
   - ☑ c. Wolfgang Amadeus Mozart
   - ☑ d. Ludwig van Beethoven
   - ☑ e. Franz Schubert
   - ☑ f. Richard Wagner
   - ☑ g. Johannes Brahms
   - ☑ h. Pyotr Ilyich Tchaikovsky

B. With a partner, check (✔) which of the elements below are metals and which elements are poisonous. Discuss your answers with your partner.

Element	… is a metal.	… is not a metal.	… is poisonous.	… is not poisonous.
1. Mercury …	☑	☐	☑	☐
2. Chlorine …	☐	☑	☑	☐
3. Oxygen …	☐	☑	☐	☑
4. Lead …	☑	☐	☑	☐
5. Iron …	☑	☐	☑	☑

2 | Active Previewing

A. Preview the academic text below. Underline the title, the first sentence of each paragraph, and the last sentence of the text as you preview.

B. Discuss the question below with a partner.

What is the topic of this text?

REMEMBER

Preview longer academic texts a second time. For more on *previewing academic texts*, see page 4.

3 | Reading and Recalling

A. Read the text. Stop after each paragraph and tell a partner two things that you remember about it.

Study Concludes Beethoven Died from Lead Poisoning

by Rick Weiss

1 Scientists believe they have collected conclusive evidence, or proof, that Ludwig van Beethoven died of lead poisoning. They used the most powerful x-ray[1] beam in the Western Hemisphere on six of the famous composer's hairs and a few pieces of his skull. The results excite scientists because they confirm earlier hints, or clues, that lead caused Beethoven's death. Beethoven had poor health for many years, and his death, in 1827 at age 56, was long and painful.

2 The tests were done at the Energy Department's Argonne National Laboratory outside Chicago. Bill Walsh and Ken Kemner headed[2] the study. Walsh is an expert in forensic[3] analysis and is chief scientist at Pfeiffer Treatment Center in Warrenville, Illinois. Kemner is a researcher at the Energy Department. Walsh said, "There's no doubt in my mind … [Beethoven] was a victim of lead poisoning."

continued

---

[1] **x-ray:** here, a special beam that can pass through solid objects

[2] **to head:** to be in charge of

[3] **forensic:** related to using science or technology to prove a fact in a court of law

continued

3 The source of Beethoven's lead poisoning is still a mystery, however. It is possible that the poisoning occurred over many years. One theory (idea) about the source is lead cups, which Beethoven drank from regularly. Another theory is that it was a lifetime of medical treatments that poisoned him. In the 19th century, medical treatments often contained heavy metals[4].

4 One metal that was clearly absent was mercury, according to Walsh. This detail weakens the theory supported by some people that Beethoven suffered from syphilis. In those days, the common treatment for this disease was mercury, which we now know is a poisonous metal. Therefore, if Beethoven had been treated for syphilis, mercury would have been present in the tests. "We found zero evidence of that," Walsh said.

5 The special x-ray machine at Argonne produces rays that are 100 times as bright as the sun. Scientists can turn those rays on tiny samples that need to be analyzed, or tested. As the x-rays hit the atoms in a sample, they cause a brief release of energy. It creates a kind of "signature" that shows what types of atoms are present.

6 The scientists discovered that many of the atoms in Beethoven's body were lead atoms. The hair sample results showed 60 parts per million. This amount is about 100 times higher than normal. The bone samples were also extremely high in lead. However, technical problems prevented the team from getting a precise, or exact, number for those samples.

7 The hair samples were from a lock (piece) of Beethoven's hair purchased by a collector from Sotheby's[5] several years ago. In 2000, scientists received two of the hairs to do some first studies. At that time, the test methods destroyed the hairs. And although the results suggested high levels of lead, there was a question about whether this was due to long-term exposure or short-term exposure.

> **REMEMBER**
> Skip the words and phrases you don't understand.

8 Because the first test methods required destroying the hairs used for the tests, the owner was not willing to give the scientists any more. Argonne's x-ray technique, however, does not destroy the materials being analyzed, so the collector agreed to the tests.

9 The pieces of Beethoven's skull belong to a California businessman. They passed through his family from a great-great-uncle, who was a doctor in Austria. The businessman wanted to compare the test results for DNA between the skull bits and the hairs first to see if the bones did, in fact, belong to Beethoven. Therefore, Walsh and Kemner had to keep secret the results of the test for lead on the skull bits for more than a year.

continued

---

[4] **heavy metal:** a metal, such as lead or mercury, that is poisonous

[5] **Sotheby's:** a famous "auction house"—a company that holds public sales of (usually expensive) objects; the person who offers to pay the most money receives the object

continued

10   William Meredith, a Beethoven scholar, believes the bones are indeed Beethoven's. Meredith is the director of the Center for Beethoven Studies at San Jose State University in San Jose, California. He says that although the tests are not 100% conclusive (positive), it is clear that the bones belonged to the famous composer.

11   Beethoven developed serious health problems in his early twenties, which grew worse over time. They reflected many of the symptoms of lead poisoning, including severe stomach problems. The composer was also deaf by his late twenties. This problem, however, may not be connected to the lead poisoning because deafness has only rarely been associated with exposure to lead. But with his many health problems, Beethoven may have been killed by the medicines he took, Meredith said. Or it is even possible that some of Beethoven's medicines absorbed, or took in, the lead contained in glass medicine bottles at the time.

12   Although the source of the lead that was in Beethoven's body is still unknown, the new research is an important contribution. Many doctors have made guesses about what the real problem was with Beethoven's health, Meredith said. This time, however, actual science is giving us the answers.

B. Read the text again without pausing. Tell your partner two new things that you remember.

C. Work as a class or in large groups. Try to name as many things as you can about the text.

4 | Understanding the Text

A. Answer as many questions as you can without looking at the text. Discuss your answers with a partner.

1. How do scientists say Beethoven died?

   a. from x-rays

   b. from lead poisoning

   c. from a disease

2. What helped scientists discover how Beethoven died?

   a. all of the medical treatments he had during his life

   b. large amounts of mercury in his blood

   c. special tests they were recently able to do

3. What did the scientists use for testing?

   a. six hairs from Beethoven's head and some bits of his skull

   b. medical records kept by Beethoven's doctors

   c. pieces of Beethoven's arm bone and stomach lining

B. Complete the sentences according to the text.

___d___ 1. For many years before he died, Beethoven had

___e___ 2. The source of the lead that was in Beethoven's body

___a___ 3. The test results showed that the levels of lead in Beethoven's body were

_b.~~g~~.___ 4. The test methods used on Beethoven's hairs in 2000

_c~~g~~~~g~~_ 5. The Argonne x-ray technique recently used on Beethoven's hairs

a. about 100 times higher than normal.

b. destroyed the hairs.

c. did not destroy the hairs.

d. poor health.

e. is still unknown.

5 | Understanding the Topic

A. Lists. Read the lists and circle the item that is the topic.

1. Warrenville   Chicago   (cities)   San Jose

2. a lifetime of medical treatments

   (possible) sources of Beethoven's lead poisoning

   the lead contained in the glass medicine bottles

   lead cups from which Beethoven drank

3. William Meredith, a Beethoven scholar

   Ken Kemner, a researcher

   (experts) who have studied the results of the lead tests on Beethoven

   Bill Walsh, a scientist and expert in forensic analysis

B. Text. Write _T_ for _Topic_, _G_ for _Too General_, and _S_ for _Too Specific_. Discuss your answers with a partner.

1. What is the topic of the text?

   a. __G__ scientific evidence about lead poisoning

   b. __T__ scientific proof that Beethoven died of lead poisoning

   c. __S__ Beethoven's long and painful death in 1827

2. Is your answer for the topic here the same as the one you determined after you previewed the text, or is your answer different? _____

C. Paragraphs. Write _T_ for _Topic_, _G_ for _Too General_, and _S_ for _Too Specific_. Discuss your answers with a partner.

1. What is the topic of ¶3?

   a. __S__ Beethoven's lead cups

   b. __G__ lead poisoning

   c. __T__ the source of Beethoven's lead poisoning

2. What is the topic of ¶5?

   a. _S_ the atoms in a sample tested by the Argonne x-ray machine

   b. _T_ the x-ray machine at Argonne

   c. _G_ x-ray machines

3. What is the topic of ¶11?

   a. _T_ Beethoven's health problems

   b. _S_ Beethoven's severe stomach problems

   c. _G_ health problems

6 | Understanding Subject and Object Pronouns

Decide what each subject or object pronoun refers to according to the text.

1. What do these pronouns refer to in ¶1?

   a. they (they have collected) _scientists_

   b. They (They used the most) _"_

   c. they (they confirm earlier) _results_

2. What do these pronouns refer to in ¶3?

   a. It (It is possible) ~~lead poisoning~~ X (insertion) b. him (that poisoned him) _Beethoven_

3. What do these pronouns refer to in ¶11?

   a. They (They reflected many) _health problems_

   b. he (the medicines he took) _Beethoven_

   c. it (it is even possible) ~~the medicines contained lead~~ X it insertion

7 | Understanding Vocabulary in Context—Synonyms

Write the synonym for each word or phrase according to the text.

1. evidence (¶1) _proof_

2. hint (¶1) _clue_

3. theory (¶3) _idea_

4. to analyze (¶5) _to test_

5. precise (¶6) _exact_

6. lock (¶7) _pice_

7. conclusive (¶10) _positive_

8. to absorb (¶11) _to take in_

8 | Discussing the Issues

Answer the questions and discuss your answers with a partner.

1. What medical treatments or medicines today (if any) might prove to be dangerous 200 years from now? Why do you think so?

2. Would you like to own some hair or bits of skull that belonged to someone famous? Why or why not?

3. Why are some people so interested in finding out how famous people have died?

Putting It On Paper

A. Write a paragraph on one of these topics.

1. Think of a musician or a composer you like. Describe what you like about this person and/or his or her work.

2. Think of a song or musical composition you like. Describe how it makes you feel (or what it makes you think about) when you listen to it.

Steps for your paragraph

a. In your first sentence, make a statement that shows which topic you are writing about.

b. In your supporting sentences, give several examples that show why.

B. Exchange paragraphs with a partner. First read your partner's paragraph and answer the questions in the checklist. Then give feedback to your partner.

✔ CHECKLIST
1. Does the first sentence clearly show which topic your partner chose?
2. Do the following sentences give examples that support or illustrate the topic?
3. Do you understand why your partner likes the musician/composer OR how your partner feels (or what he/she thinks about) when listening to the music?
4. Is there any information in the paragraph that is not related to your partner's topic? If yes, please underline it on your partner's paper, and write it below:

_____

_____

_____

_____

_____

_____

_____

_____

_____

C. Revise your paragraph based on your partner's feedback.

Taking It Online | Music-Makers

A. With a partner, use the Internet to research one female musician or composer and one male musician or composer.

1. Use Google (www.google.com) or another major search engine to find Websites with information about two of the following musicians or composers:

Ayumi Hamasaki	Irving Berlin	Rolando Villazón
Edith Piaf	Johnny Cash	Saburo Kitajima
Elvis Presley	Khaled	Shakira
Faye Wong	Oum Kalthoum	Yo-Yo Ma

2. Preview the Websites as you would a magazine article or an essay.

B. Complete the tables with the information you find.

Music-Maker: Ludwig van Beethoven	
Website address: www.somewhere.com	✔ Man
When he or she was born: 1770 Nationality: German	☐ Woman
Kind of music: Western classical	☐ Musician
One interesting fact: He began to lose his hearing in his late 20s, but he composed wonderful music even after he was completely deaf.	✔ Composer

Music-Maker:	
Website address:	☐ Man
When he or she was born: Nationality:	☐ Woman
Kind of music:	☐ Musician
One interesting fact:	☐ Composer

Music-Maker:	
Website address:	☐ Man
When he or she was born: Nationality:	☐ Woman
Kind of music:	☐ Musician
One interesting fact:	☐ Composer

C. **Following Up. Tell your classmates the facts you discovered. See if they can guess which musician or composer you researched.**

The Sociology of Food

Answer the questions and briefly discuss your answers with a partner.

1. Do you prefer eating at home or eating in a restaurant?

2. What are the people in the photos doing?

3. How important do you think food is in a culture?

aphrodisiac.

Text 1 | Lost in the Kitchen

1 | Getting Started

A. Answer the questions and briefly discuss your answers with a partner.

1. Do you know how to cook?

2. Do you think it is important for people to know how to cook? Why or why not?

3. If someone wanted to learn how to cook, what could she or he do?

B. Check (✔) the number of times per week that you do the following.

Eating habits	0-1 time	2-3 times	4 or more times
1. I eat meals prepared and cooked at home.	☐	☐	☐
2. I eat store-bought meals that are reheated at home.	☐	☐	☐
3. I eat foods that have been prepared by a restaurant at home.	☐	☐	☐

READING SKILL Previewing Newspaper Articles

Newspaper articles usually order information from the most important to the least important. The first two to four paragrahps usually answer the questions *Who? What? When? Where?* The rest of the article gives the details. To **preview** a newspaper article:

1. Read the title.

2. Look at any photos and read the captions.

3. Read the first two to four paragraphs.

2 | Active Previewing

A. Preview the newspaper article on the next page by reading the first two paragraphs. Then answer the questions with a partner.

1. Who doesn't know cooking basics today?

2. What is the Culinary Institute of America?

3. When does it offer courses to home cooks?

4. Where (in which city) is the Culinary Institute of America?

B. Answer this question with a partner.

What is the topic of this newspaper article?

3 | Reading and Recalling

A. Read the text. Stop after each paragraph and tell a partner two things that you remember about it.

Despite the Growing Popularity of "Food Culture," Many Can't Cook

BY MICHAEL HILL

1   Even as American "food culture" grows, many adults in the United States today simply don't know cooking basics. Cooking basics are simple kitchen skills, such as chopping, baking, and boiling. People who lack these simple skills are at a true disadvantage in the kitchen.

2   The Culinary[1] Institute of America (known as the "CIA") is a famous training school for cooks and is located in Hyde Park, NY. This training can take up to several years to complete; however, the CIA also offers short classes to home cooks on weekends.

3   On a weekend when other kitchen classrooms are packed[2] with adults who are learning to prepare <u>complex</u> meals, Chef Greg Zifchak is teaching his class of 15 students very simple cooking techniques.

4   The class is called "Cook's Skill Development," and the students follow his directions with uneven results. They make a lot of mistakes and often ask questions that even beginning cooks know the answers to. They belong to the "lost-in-the-kitchen generation."

5   The lost-in-the-kitchen <u>generation</u> describes the many adults of today who never learned even the simplest cooking techniques from their parents. As families began eating together less often, many people grew up never learning the basics in the kitchen.

Training schools offer basic cooking courses for beginners.

6   John Nihoff, a professor of gastronomy[3] at the Culinary Institute, studies food culture. He claims that when society became more work-oriented in the '60s, Mom was more likely to work outside the home, and workdays for both parents got longer.

continued

---

[1] **culinary:** having to do with cooking

[2] **to be packed:** to be filled

[3] **gastronomy:** the study of good food and eating

continued

7   Because of this change in families' working schedules, people now eat much more convenience food than they used to. Convenience food is food that has already been prepared and just needs to be reheated and eaten. According to Nihoff, the reason that families have become increasingly dependent on it is because they cook less and less.

8   Traditionally, Mom passed on cooking skills. However, this tradition is now suffering, Nihoff said. He notes that Americans now spend $121 billion a year on "home meal replacements." Home meal replacements are partially or fully cooked dinners that are bought in restaurants or supermarkets and then eaten at home.

9   Chef Zifchak frequently comes across[4] adults who have no kitchen skills. None of the students in his recent skills class handled knives correctly, for example. And he noticed students seemed very impressed when he demonstrated how to sauté—pan fry—fish. However, he says the technique is very simple: "All I did was heat up oil and put a piece of fish in the pan."

10   Because of his students' limited knowledge, Zifchak only explains simple kitchen tips to them: Don't overstir while caramelizing (browning) onions; baste a lot for successful browning; don't lean on the stove, as it is "very dangerous."

11   Cooking is not just a quaint—or old-fashioned—skill, but an important family tradition that encourages more healthful eating, says Lisa Young.

Young is a nutritionist and author of *The Portion Teller*.

12   Instead of baking potatoes and broiling fish, parents are bringing home French fries and deep-fried fish. A main diet of fast food can lead to long-term health problems, such as obesity and heart disease, she notes.

13   The danger is that this problem will get worse over time. Parents without kitchen skills only pass on take-out-ordering skills to their children. But Nihoff sees signs of change. There is a renewed interest in fresh, wholesome food, for example. Furthermore, when people settle down to bring up families, many are showing an interest in cooking, Nihoff says.

14   Information about learning to cook is available through many sources. Cookbooks are big business. Television food programs are on 24-7[5], and there is a rapidly growing number of culinary courses available—such as the day-long course offered at the CIA.

15   Despite the intense heat and rushing around, students are happy. As one person put it: "It's exciting to be a real chef."

> **REMEMBER**
> Skip the words and phrases you do not understand.

---

[4] **to come across:** to meet by chance
[5] **24-7:** 24 hours a day, seven days a week

B. Read the text again without pausing. Tell your partner two new things that you remember.

C. Work as a class or in large groups. Try to name as many things as you can about the text.

4 | Understanding the Text

A. Answer as many questions as you can without looking at the text. Discuss your answers with a partner.

1. According to the text, many American adults nowadays:

    a. have better cooking skills than their parents did.

    (b.) don't know cooking basics.

    c. learned how to cook from their grandparents.

2. What does Chef Zifchak teach the adults?

    (a.) simple cooking techniques

    b. cake-decorating techniques

    c. advanced cooking techniques

3. According to the text, what do many Americans nowadays eat?

    a. less convenience food than they did before

    (b.) more convenience food than they did before

    c. the same amount of convenience food as they did before

B. Write *T* for *True* and *F* for *False* according to the text. Discuss your answers with a partner.

____F____ 1. Even as American "food culture" expands, many adults in the United States today understand more and more about cooking.

____T____ 2. The students in Chef Zifchak's class make a lot of mistakes.

____F____ 3. As families began eating together less often, many people grew up knowing a lot about cooking basics.

____T____ 4. John Nihoff claims that many people now rely on "home meal replacements."

____F____ 5. Not very much information about learning to cook is available.

5 | Understanding the Topic

Write *T* for *Topic*, *G* for *Too General*, and *S* for *Too Specific*. Discuss your answers with a partner.

1. What is the topic of the text?

    a. ____T____ American adults who are learning cooking skills

    b. ____G____ cooking skills

    c. ____S____ American adults who are learning how to use kitchen knives

2. Is your answer for the topic here the same as the one you determined after you previewed the text, or is your answer different? _____

Sometimes a writer explains unfamiliar words by writing the **definition**. In a text, definitions are often indicated by verbs such as *be, mean, refer to, describe,* and *be called.*

Read the following sentence.

Cooking basics *are* simple kitchen skills, such as chopping, baking, and boiling. (¶1)

What are *cooking basics*? The verb *are (be)* introduces the definition: *simple kitchen skills.*

6 | Understanding Vocabulary in Context—Definitions

Write the definition for each word or phrase according to the text. Discuss your answers with a partner.

1. the lost-in-the-kitchen generation (¶5) Many adults who never learned even simple cooking skills.

2. convenience food (¶7) the food that have already prepared

3. home meal replacement (¶8) partially, or fully cooked dinners.

7 | Discussing the Issues

Answer the questions and discuss your answers with a partner.

1. Do you think it is important for parents to pass on cooking skills to their children? Why or why not?

2. Do you think it is important for people to eat home-cooked food? Why or why not?

3. In your opinion, what are the advantages and disadvantages of learning how to cook your own meals?

Text 2 | Table Manners

1 | Getting Started

A. Check (✔) the behaviors that you consider polite and not polite. Discuss your answers with a partner.

Behavior	Polite	Not polite
1. chewing or eating with your mouth open	☐	☑
2. putting your elbows on the table while you eat	☑	☐
3. taking the biggest piece of food	☐	☑
4. making noises with your mouth while you eat or drink	☑	☐
5. refusing food that is offered to you	☐	☑

B. Complete the chart. What other dining behaviors are polite or not polite in your family?

Polite
1.
2.
3.

Not polite
1.
2.
3.

2 | Active Previewing

Preview the magazine article on the next page. Underline the title, the first sentence of each paragraph, and the last sentence of the text as you preview. Then answer this question with a partner.

What is the topic of this text?

3 | Reading and Recalling

A. Read the text. Stop after each paragraph and tell a partner two things that you remember about it.

Food Faux Pas

BY TERRI MORRISON

1 ### Everyone Makes Mistakes

Everyone has made a mistake or two at the dining table. Whether we knock over a glass of milk when we're 4 years old, or use the wrong fork when we're 40 years old, we all sometimes break dining rules. These embarrassing dining mistakes are called food "faux pas."

2 For example, while I was at a formal dinner in Paris, I unconsciously placed my left hand in my lap—the polite thing to do in the United States but wrong in France. The French keep both hands gracefully balanced on the table's edge, and of course, they hold the fork in the left hand and the knife in the right. My improper behavior at this very lovely dinner disturbed the gentleman to my left so much that he took hold of my left hand and placed it upon the table. It surprised me, but I sure kept my hands where they belonged for the rest of that meal!

3 ### How to Be a Good Host

Taboo behavior is behavior that is forbidden or should not be done. When traveling around the world, it can be difficult to remember which behaviors are taboo and which behaviors are appropriate (correct). However, it can be just as difficult to host visitors from other countries.

4 Nancy Gilboy, the executive director of the International Visitors Council in Philadelphia, Pennsylvania, constantly hosts delegations[1] from all over the world. Therefore, Gilboy must be careful to avoid various food taboos (never serve pork to Muslims, beef to Hindus, etc.). She has also noted that people in certain cultures are careful to make sure that everyone receives an equal share of the meal.

5 When shrimp was passed around at a dinner with a group from China, Gilboy took three or four and offered it to the next diner. Subsequently, she noticed that each attendee took just one shrimp in turn and offered it to the next person. In Chinese culture, it is important to make sure the other diners get enough to eat, so the Chinese often take a single portion of food at a time.

6 ### Good Eats?

Some people's food preferences are constrained, or limited. If you have religious, ethical, or medical guidelines, or rules, of course you must follow them. But be sure to tell your hosts before they spend time and money preparing a special, totally unpalatable[2] local delicacy[3] for you. Turning down caviar[4] and champagne in Bulgaria, Romania, or Russia can be the equivalent of throwing away a month of your hosts' wages.

REMEMBER
Skip the words and phrases you do not understand.

7 In many parts of the world, people only do business with those they know and trust, and that kind of contact is generally established, or started, over lunch or dinner. When international executives visit clients in countries like Brazil or Chile, they often try to get their appointments around 11 a.m., so they can all go to lunch together afterward. They spend time in a friendly environment, where no business is discussed, but friendships and trust are established. Bringing business up too soon (if at all) over a meal in Spain, France, or China can ruin a future business relationship.

8 However, even the most cultured diner on earth can become involved in unfortunate situations. The queen of England, who is polite enough to try almost anything, was the center of attention after a visit to Belize. During her visit, the queen ate a local delicacy, a dibnut. A dibnut is an animal that looks like a large chipmunk[5]. When the English press found out what the queen had been served, the headlines ran "Queen Eats Rat!" Fortunately, citizens of Belize have a sense of humor and immediately changed the dish from "dibnut" on their menus to "Royal Rat."

9 Whether you're eating rat or roe, enjoy the ambiance (environment) and try to copy the local rules for dining.

---

[1] **delegation:** a person or a group of persons that officially represent another person or group of persons

[2] **unpalatable:** not delicious; not pleasant

[3] **delicacy:** a rare and special food

[4] **caviar:** fish eggs, also called *roe*

[5] **chipmunk:** a small animal, similar to a squirrel, that lives underground

B. Read the text again without pausing. Tell your partner two new things that you remember.

C. Work as a class or in large groups. Try to name as many things as you can about the text.

4 | Understanding the Text

A. Answer as many questions as you can without looking at the text. Discuss your answers with a partner.

1. What is true about dining rules?

   a. All cultures have the same rules.

   b. The rules may be different from culture to culture.

   c. Dining rules are not important.

2. According to the text, who breaks dining rules?

   a. people who tell their hosts about their food preferences

   b. only some people do

   c. everyone does

3. According to the text, what is a good rule to follow when one is in another culture?

   a. to sit next to the host

   b. to eat the foods that one's hosts offer

   c. to try to copy the local rules for dining

B. Which of the three photos do you think could best accompany the text? Discuss your answer with a partner.

5 | Understanding the Topic

A. Text. Write *T* for *Topic, G* for *Too General*, and *S* for *Too Specific*. **Discuss your answers with a partner.**

1. What is the topic of the text?

   a. __T__ food faux pas

   b. __G__ food

   c. __S__ French food faux pas

2. Is your answer for the topic here the same as the one you determined after you previewed the text, or is your answer different? _____

B. Paragraphs. Write *T* for *Topic, G* for *Too General*, and *S* for *Too Specific*. **Discuss your answers with a partner.**

1. What is the topic of ¶2?

   a. _____ French dining

   b. _____ how to hold the fork properly in France

   c. _____ example of a food faux pas at a dinner in France

2. What is the topic of ¶6?

   a. _____ turning down food in Bulgaria

   b. _____ food preferences

   c. _____ telling one's hosts about food preferences

3. What is the topic of ¶7?

   a. _____ developing trusting business relationships over meals in some foreign countries

   b. _____ lunch in some countries

   c. _____ having lunch with clients in Brazil or Chile

6 | Understanding Subject and Object Pronouns

Write the subject or object that the pronoun refers to according to the text. Discuss your answers with a partner.

1. they (they hold the fork) (¶2) _the French_

2. he (he took hold of my left hand) (¶2) _the gentleman_

3. it (it can be difficult) (¶3) _(no specific)_

4. she (she has also noted) (¶4) _Nancy Grilboy_

5. she (Subsequently, she noticed) (¶5) _" (Grilboy)_

6. they (before they spend time) (¶6) _your hosts._

7. they (with those they know and trust) (¶7) _people_

8. they (they often try to get their appointments around 11 a.m.) (¶7) _international executives_

Phrasal verbs are verbs combined with particles such as *in, out, up, down, through, over,* and *onto.* When a verb is combined with a particle, it can have a different meaning from the verb and/or particle itself. Use the surrounding context to help you understand the meaning of phrasal verbs.

Read the following sentence.

Whether we *knock over* a glass of milk when we're 4 years old, or use the wrong fork when we're 40 years old, we all sometimes break dining rules. (¶1)

We know that we do not plan to hit a glass of milk (as we would *knock on,* or hit, a door). However, we do know that mistakes at the dinner table could include spilling or dropping things. Together, the verb *to knock* and the particle *over* make a phrasal verb that means *to spill* or *overturn* something so that it falls.

7 | Understanding Vocabulary in Context

A. Phrasal Verbs. Select the best definition for each phrasal verb. Discuss your answers with a partner.

1. to pass around (¶5)

   a. to cook   b. to pass from one person to another   c. to discuss quietly

2. to turn down (¶6)

   a. to buy   b. to refuse   c. to eat, consume

3. to throw away (¶6)

   a. to waste   b. to pay   c. to ask for

4. to bring up (¶7)

   a. to worry   b. to introduce into a conversation   c. to get an appointment

5. to find out (¶8)

   a. to believe   b. to discover, learn   c. to read

B. Definitions. Write the definition for each word or phrase according to the text. Discuss your answers with a partner.

1. food "faux pas" (¶1) _embarrassing dining mistakes_

2. taboo behavior (¶3) _behavior that is forbidden or should not be done._

3. dibnut (¶8) _an a_

C. Synonyms. Write the synonym for each word or phrase according to the text. Discuss your answers with a partner.

1. appropriate (¶3) _____

2. constrained (¶6) _____

3. guidelines (¶6) _____

4. established (¶7) _____

5. ambiance (¶9) _____

8 | Discussing the Issues

Answer the questions and discuss your answers with a partner.

1. What food faux pas have you committed or seen someone commit?

2. What food faux pas bother or annoy people in your family? Why?

3. In your opinion, is it important to follow rules about food and dining? Why or why not?

Text 3 | Order Up!

1 | Getting Started

Answer the questions and briefly discuss your answers with a partner.

1. Do you like to eat in restaurants?

2. How often do you eat at a restaurant?

3. What do you do when you go to a restaurant with friends? Check (✔) all that apply.

☐ a. check the prices

☐ b. look at the menu

☐ c. order something new and different

☐ d. order something you've ordered before

☐ e. read everything on the menu

☐ f. share the bill equally

Graphics Previewing Menus and Price Lists

Menus and other **price lists** are usually divided into categories. **Preview** menus and price lists by reading the category titles (*Side Orders, Soup, Salad, Chili,* etc.) and any information that is printed in large letters. Then focus on any details that catch your eye.

2 | Active Previewing

Preview the menu below and then answer the questions. Discuss your answers with a partner.

1. What is the name of this restaurant?

2. What four categories are on the menu?

   a. _____   b. _____   c. _____   d. _____

3. Check (✔) the food you think is served at this restaurant.

   ☐ a. Japanese   ☐ c. Mexican   ☐ e. Thai

   ☐ b. Middle Eastern   ☐ d. North American   ☐ f. Italian

Open Mon-Sun
11:00AM-9:00PM

Soquel 476-6260
Santa Cruz 427-1800

Carpo's Restaurant

BURGERS AND SANDWICHES

CARPO BURGER
1/2 lb. Black Angus ground chuck,
on a sourdough baguette $4.95

REGULAR BURGER
6 oz. Black Angus ground chuck, on a sesame bun $4.25

CARPO HOT DOG
Grilled 1/4 lb. all-beef frank served on a sesame bun $3.75

REGULAR HOT DOG
Same as the Carpo Dog, just smaller $2.75

GRILLED CHICKEN SANDWICH
Skinless, boneless chicken breast on a whole wheat bun, topped with grilled onions and cheese $5.75

GRILLED CHEESE SANDWICH
Simple, but good!! Cheddar cheese on sourdough bread $3.75

SOUP, SALAD, CHILI

HOMEMADE SOUP
A 12 oz. bowl of our freshly-prepared soup served with fresh bread and butter. $3.25

SALAD BAR
Build your own!! Our dressings are homemade and use only the freshest ingredients. $5.95

SOUP & SALAD BAR
Try one of our homemade soups along with our salad bar for a great meal. $7.50

CLASSIC HOMEMADE CHILI
A 12 oz. bowl. A special recipe! $3.75

SIDE ORDERS
FRESH-CUT FRIES • ONION RINGS • VEGETABLES/PASTA

BEVERAGES AND SHAKES
SODAS • ICED TEA • LEMONADE • MILK
HOT TEA • COFFEE • MILKSHAKES

---

3 | Scanning

Scan the menu for the answers to the questions. Discuss your answers with a partner.

1. What is the phone number of the Santa Cruz Carpo's? _427-1800_

2. Which is smaller: the Carpo Hot Dog or the Regular Hot Dog? _____

3. How many ounces (oz.) of homemade soup are in a bowl? _____

4. How much does the salad bar cost? _____

5. Which sandwich costs $5.75? _____

6. What are the restaurant's hours? _____

7. Which is more expensive: a bowl of soup or a bowl of chili? _____

8. Does the restaurant sell French fries? _____

4 | Discussing the Issues

Answer the questions and discuss your answers with a partner.

1. Do you like the kind of food described in the menu on page 57? Why or why not?

2. What is your favorite kind of restaurant? Why?

3. What are some of the advantages and disadvantages of eating in a restaurant?

Text 4 | Food Aromas

1 | Getting Started

A. Answer the questions and briefly discuss your answers with a partner.

1. Do you like any deep-fried foods?

2. Are there any dishes from your hometown or region that others consider to be strange? If so, what are they?

3. Do you enjoy trying food that is sold on the street? Why or why not?

B. Check (✔) the statements about food you enjoy. Discuss your answers with a partner.

☐ **1.** It should contain only fresh ingredients.

☐ **2.** It should taste good.

☐ **3.** It should look appealing or attractive.

☐ **4.** It should smell good.

☐ **5.** Everyone should enjoy it.

☐ **6.** It should smell strong.

2 | Active Previewing

Preview the academic text on the next page. Underline the title, the first sentence of each paragraph, and the last sentence of the text as you preview. Then answer this question with a partner.

What is the topic of this text?

> **REMEMBER**
> Preview longer academic texts a second time.

3 | Reading and Recalling

A. Read the text. Stop after each paragraph and tell a partner two things that you remember about it.

Deliciously Stinky

Chinese stinky tofu: love it or hate it, there's no ignoring it.

by Stephen Jack

1   "Stinky tofu" is such a notorious[1] dish that it seems strange that I cannot remember my own first experience with it. What I do remember, though, is my father's reaction when he first discovered it. He and my brother were visiting me in Taiwan, and we were doing a brief tour of the island. We were in Tainan, a city that is famous for its temples.

2   I was unfolding my map as we walked down the street, when my father stopped and spun around in panic[2]. "God, what's that smell?" I pointed to a stinky tofu vendor[3], the acrid (sour) smoke floating around his pushcart. "That's what they call stinky tofu. Want to try some?"

3   Actually, it was a silly question. My dad walked quickly away. He didn't slow down until he was safely away from me and the stinky tofu stand and was sure that he wasn't being followed.

4   Tofu is bean curd paste. In its basic form, tofu is a bland (flavorless) food. So what puts the stink into stinky tofu? For this, a fermenting brine is needed. A fermenting brine is a salty and flavorful soaking liquid. Traditionally, the brine for stinky tofu includes vegetables and shrimp and is made in a very large uncovered earthenware jar. The mixture is left to sit for up to six months while microorganisms go to work. The finished product is so strong that the tasteless white cubes of tofu are transformed, or changed, into something that smells terrifying after just four to six hours in the brine. The tofu is then rinsed and aged overnight in the refrigerator before it is ready to be cooked.

5   Stinky tofu is widely available in China, but in Taiwan it is especially popular. In Taiwan, stinky tofu is normally deep-fried. It should be golden and crisp, even crusty. It is served with a spicy topping that nicely complements[4] the tofu. Once the cubes of tofu are fried and drained, the vendor gently makes a hole in the top of each cube with a chopstick or tongs. This action lets the topping penetrate, or soak into, the tofu. The topping is crucial—necessary—to the dish. It consists of vinegar, sesame oil, shredded oriental cucumber, and pickled Chinese cabbage. After the topping, the tofu receives a splash of chili sauce and some minced garlic. The strong odor is mainly in the cooking, and it subsides, or weakens, once the tofu comes out of the oil.

6   Stinky tofu is normally a street food. As the name suggests, street food is food that is sold on the street. (With stinky tofu, there is a good reason for this. If someone tries to cook this dish at home, he or she will be asked to move out immediately—not just from the house, but from the neighborhood!) The stinky tofu vendor will rent a space in a night market or set up a few folding tables by the side of a busy road and cook from a stove set on the back of a small truck. Late in the afternoon he fires up his oil-filled wok and drops in five large cubes of tofu. Within seconds a strange, highly pungent[5] odor fills the air, attacking the nose of anyone who is close enough to smell it. The vendor has no need for fancy signs or loudspeakers to sell his product. There are many devotees, or fans, of stinky tofu,

continued

> **REMEMBER**
> Skip the words and phrases you do not understand.

---

[1] **notorious:** well-known but usually unfavorably *adj. (infamous)*
[2] **panic:** sudden and extreme fear
[3] **vendor:** a person who sells something *street vendor.*
[4] **to complement:** to go well with
[5] **pungent:** sharp, strong

continued

and they will be attracted by the <u>unmistakable</u> smell. Everyone else will run like crazy, which is basically what my dad did in Tainan.

7   Few restaurants will serve stinky tofu, and those that do are likely to be specialists: stinky tofu restaurants only sell stinky tofu. Since all the clients come to eat the same thing, no one can be offended, or annoyed. These restaurants usually prepare stinky tofu in many different ways, such as deep-fried, stewed, steamed, or even raw.

8   Stinky tofu is also known as "smelly tofu." But "smelly" doesn't seem to be a strong enough adjective to describe the power of this dish. Stinky tofu has a smell that cannot be described or imagined. In order to believe it, one must experience it.

9   I now live in Taiwan and have developed a taste for stinky tofu. In fact, it has become one of my favorite street snacks. My brother has never visited me in Taiwan again, and my father did not return for years. Nothing has ever been said, but I wonder if memories of stinky tofu in Tainan had something to do with that.

B. Read the text again without pausing. Tell your partner two new things that you remember.

C. Work as a class or in large groups. Try to name as many things as you can about the text.

④ Understanding the Text

A. Answer as many questions as you can without looking at the text. Discuss your answers with a partner.

1. How did the author's father react to the smell of stinky tofu?

  a. He wanted to try the stinky tofu.

  b. He ran away.

  c. He started to laugh.

2. How does stinky tofu become stinky?

  a. It develops its strong odor while it is cooking.

  b. It is mixed with garlic and other strong herbs.

  c. It is soaked in a fermenting brine for four to six hours.

3. Stinky tofu is normally:

  a. a street food.

  b. a home-cooked meal.

  c. a food served in all restaurants.

B. Circle the word or phrase in parentheses that best finishes each sentence. Discuss your answers with a partner.

1. In its basic form, tofu is normally (flavorless/stinky).

2. Stinky tofu is especially popular in (Taiwan/Japan).

3. The odor of stinky tofu becomes (stronger/weaker) after cooking.

4. (Almost no one/Many people) enjoy(s) stinky tofu.

5. There (is only one way/are many ways) to serve stinky tofu.

⑤ | Understanding the Topic

A. Text. Write *T* for *Topic, G* for *Too General,* and *S* for *Too Specific.* **Discuss your answers with a partner.**

1. What is the topic of the text?

a. ___G___ tofu

b. ___T___ stinky tofu

c. ___S___ stinky tofu vendors

2. Is your answer for the topic here the same as the one you determined after you previewed the text, or is your answer different? _____

B. Paragraphs. Write *T* for *Topic, G* for *Too General,* and *S* for *Too Specific.* **Discuss your answers with a partner.**

1. What is the topic of ¶**4**?

a. ___G___ tofu

b. ___S___ the fermenting brine for stinky tofu

c. ___T___ how stinky tofu is made

2. What is the topic of ¶**5**?

a. ___S___ deep-frying stinky tofu

b. ___T___ how stinky tofu is served

c. ___G___ stinky tofu

3. What is the topic of ¶**7**?

a. ___T___ restaurants that serve stinky tofu

b. ___G___ restaurants

c. ___S___ ways that restaurants prepare stinky tofu

⑥ | Understanding Subject and Object Pronouns

Write the subject or object that the pronoun refers to according to the text. Briefly discuss your answers with a partner.

1. What do these pronouns refer to in ¶**1**?

a. it (it seems strange) _it insertion_____

b. it (my own first experience with it) ____Stinky tofu_____

c. he (he first discovered) _____father_____

2. What do these pronouns refer to in ¶5?

    a. it (it is especially popular) _____ *stanky tofo* _____

    b. It (It consists of) _____ *topping* _____

    c. it (it subsides, or weakens) _____ *strong odor* _____

3. What do these pronouns refer to in ¶6?

    a. he or she (he or she will be asked to move out) _____ *someone* _____

    b. he (he fires up) _____ *veador* _____

    c. it (close enough to smell it) _____ *highly pungent odor* _____

    d. they (they will be attracted by) _____ *farsor devotees* _____

7 | Understanding Vocabulary in Context

A. Definitions. Write the definition for each word or phrase according to the text. Discuss your answers with a partner.

1. tofu (¶4) _bean curd paste_

2. fermenting brine (¶4) _____

3. street food (¶6) _____

B. Synonyms. Write the synonym for each word or phrase according to the text. Discuss your answers with a partner.

1. acrid (¶2) _sour_

2. bland (¶4) _____

3. to transform (¶4) _____

4. penetrate (¶5) _____

5. crucial (¶5) _____

6. to subside (¶5) _____

7. devotee (¶6) _____

8. to be offended (¶7) _____

8 | Discussing the Issues

Answer the questions and discuss your answers with a partner.

1. Would you try or have you ever tried a dish that smelled bad but that other people said was delicious? Why or why not?

2. Do you enjoy trying unusual dishes? Why or why not?

3. Do you think people should try new dishes when they travel to a different country? Why or why not?

Putting It On Paper

A. Write a paragraph on one of these topics.

1. Describe a dish that you enjoy. What is in it, and what makes you enjoy it?

2. Describe an embarrassing experience you have had at a meal, either at someone's house or at a restaurant.

Steps for your paragraph

a. In your first sentence, make a statement that shows which topic you are writing about.

b. In your supporting sentences, give several examples that show details about the dish or the embarrassing experience.

B. Exchange paragraphs with a partner. First read your partner's paragraph and answer the questions in the checklist. Then give feedback to your partner.

✔ CHECKLIST
1. Does the first sentence clearly show the topic?
2. Do the sentences that follow give examples that support or illustrate the topic?
3. Do you understand why your partner enjoys the dish, or why your partner was embarrassed?
4. Is there any information in the paragraph that is not related to your partner's topic? If yes, please underline it on your partner's paper, and write it below:

_____

_____

_____

_____

_____

_____

C. Revise your paragraph based on your partner's feedback.

Taking It Online | Time to Eat

A. With a partner, use the Internet to research two restaurants.

1. Use Google (www.google.com) or another major search engine to find Websites with English-language menus for two restaurants. (Consider searching for "restaurant menu.")

2. Preview the Websites as you would a magazine article.

B. Complete the tables with the information you find.

ONLINE TIP

Try your search on different search engines, as each search engine might give different results.

Restaurant: Carpo's		
Website address: www.carposrestaurant.com		
Location(s): Santa Cruz, California, and Soquel, California		
Kind of food: American Type of restaurant: ☑ informal ☐ formal		
Price range: ☑ under $10 ☐ $10-$25 ☐ $25 and up		
Two menu categories: Sandwiches, Broiled Specials		

Restaurant:		
Website address:		
Location(s):		
Kind of food: Type of restaurant: ☐ informal ☐ formal		
Price range: ☐ under $10 ☐ $10-$25 ☐ $25 and up		
Two menu categories:		

Restaurant:		
Website address:		
Location(s):		
Kind of food: Type of restaurant: ☐ informal ☐ formal		
Price range: ☐ under $10 ☐ $10-$25 ☐ $25 and up		
Two menu categories:		

C. Following up. Print out the menu from one of your restaurants. Write five scanning questions about your menu and see if your classmates can find the answers.

Temporary Art

Answer the questions and briefly discuss your answers with a partner.

1. Do you enjoy art?

2. What are the people in the photos doing?

3. Do you think that doing art is a good way to express your feelings? Why or why not?

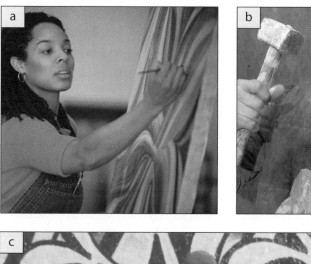

Text 1 | Art on the Beach

1 | Getting Started

A. Answer the questions and briefly discuss your answers with a partner.

1. Do you like to go to the beach?

2. Have you ever done the activity pictured in the photos? If so, describe the experience.

3. What are these creations called?

B. Check (✔) whether you agree or disagree with each statement. Briefly discuss your answers with a partner.

I think that art ...	Agree	Disagree
1. ... should last for a long time.	☐	☐
2. ... can be messy or dirty to do.	☐	☐
3. ... should be shown in a museum.	☐	☐
4. ... should be serious.	☐	☐
5. ... should be created by professionals.	☐	☐

2 | Active Previewing

A. Preview the newspaper article on the next page by reading the first two paragraphs. Then answer these questions with a partner.

1. Who is this text about?

2. What does he make?

3. Where does he do it?

4. When did he start doing it?

> **REMEMBER**
> Preview newspaper articles by reading the title, looking at any photos and reading their captions, and reading the first two to four paragraphs.
> For more on *previewing newspaper articles*, see page 46.

B. Answer these questions with a partner.

1. What is the topic of this text?

2. What is the most important thing the author wants you to know about the topic?

3 | Reading and Recalling

A. Read the text. Stop after each paragraph and tell a partner two things that you remember about it.

Sand Castles—Amazing Design, Temporary Art

BY EMILY LINDQUIST

1   It all started about ten years ago—innocently, as most sand castles do. Chad Reed made one of his first sand castles using only the basics: sand, his hands, and a desire to create. Somehow, though, the outcome[1] was not as fantastic as he had imagined.

2   The next summer, Reed returned to Block Island. He was determined to recreate the picture in his mind. He brought some beach essentials: a pail, a shovel, and his experience from the summer before. This time, his castle was closer to what he wanted but still not quite as large or detailed as the one in his imagination.

3   Finally Reed learned. The third year he brought several gadgets, including a green plastic beach pail, a large triangle-shaped pallet knife, a garden trowel, a small metal shovel, some plastic putty knives, a dandelion weed digger, and "some plastic jobby" he found at the 99-cent store. "If you want to do grand civic works[2] you have to have tools," he joked.

4   Since then, Reed has reconstructed sand versions of major landmarks from around the world, such as the Eiffel Tower, Notre Dame, and the Hagia Sophia. The aqueducts he creates are a big crowd pleaser, and he tries to incorporate[3] them when he can. Reed says he hasn't recreated any ancient Egyptian monuments yet, such as the pyramids or the Sphinx, but he believes he will soon. In the meantime, the Hanging Gardens of Babylon may be next up on his castle agenda[4]. Reed's son Devin encouraged him to use seaweed for the gardens. Reed agreed this was a great idea.

5   Working with the tide[5], Reed knows his creations will be destroyed eventually. He doesn't mind, though. He even thinks it adds to the charm of making sand castles. He works far enough away from the water to avoid early destruction but close enough to use it when needed. Devin helps by digging up mountains of sand. Working from these piles, Reed packs the sand down with water, giving the sand weight, and then begins carving away.

6   When Devin asks Reed what part of the sand castle he is making next, Reed replies, "I don't know yet. The sand tells me when I'm done." Excited by details, Reed likes to play with the sunlight — building windows and doorways with curves that wait for the golden hour of sunset, truly bringing the work to life.

7   Reed has a degree in industrial design, a field that focuses on improving the artistic and practical features of objects. Because he spends his days working in a small office, he finds that building sand castles helps him to relax.

8   Building sand castles also allows Reed to use his background in industrial design to construct while creating from nature. He likes to expand his imagination and build castles on a large scale. As Reed puts it: "Go big or stay home."

---

[1] **outcome:** result, finished project

[2] **civic work:** work that is helpful to a community

[3] **to incorporate:** to include

[4] **agenda:** a plan, a schedule

[5] **tide:** the rise and fall of the ocean, caused by the pull of the moon

B. Read the text again without pausing. Tell your partner two new things that you remember.

C. Work as a class or in large groups. Try to name as many things as you can about the text.

4 | Understanding the Text

A. Answer as many questions as you can without looking at the text. Discuss your answers with a partner.

1. When does Chad Reed build sand castles at the beach?

   a. in the spring

   b. on summer vacations

   c. before going to work

2. Who helps Reed at the beach?

   a. his brother

   b. his wife

   c. his son

3. Why does Reed enjoy making his beach art?

   a. it helps him to relax

   b. so he can win a competition

   c. to destroy it after he's finished

B. Check (✔) the statements that are true about Chad Reed and his sand castles.

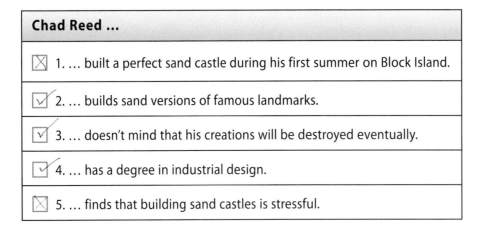

Chad Reed ...
☒ 1. ... built a perfect sand castle during his first summer on Block Island.
☑ 2. ... builds sand versions of famous landmarks.
☑ 3. ... doesn't mind that his creations will be destroyed eventually.
☑ 4. ... has a degree in industrial design.
☒ 5. ... finds that building sand castles is stressful.

The **main idea** of a text or paragraph is the most important idea the writer wants to say about the topic of that text or paragraph. The main idea is always expressed as a complete sentence. To identify the main idea:

1. Choose the idea closest to the most important idea of the whole paragraph or text.

2. Do not choose an idea that is too general.

3. Do not choose an idea that focuses on a specific detail of the paragraph or text.

Reread ¶1 on page 67. The topic is *Chad Reed's first sand castles*. The possible choices for the main idea are

      a. Chad Reed builds sand castles.

      b. Chad Reed's first sand castle was not very good.

      c. Chad Reed made one of his first sand castles using only the basics.

Choice *a* is too general to be a good main idea. This sentence refers to all of Chad Reed's sand castles, not just his first ones.

Choice *b* is too specific to be a good main idea. The paragraph is about how Chad started making sand castles, not only what happened when he built his first sand castle.

Choice *c* is the best main idea for ¶1.

5 | Understanding the Topic and Main Idea

A. Text. Write T for *Topic*, G for *Too General*, and S for *Too Specific*. Discuss your answers with a partner.

1. What is the topic of the text?

    a. ___*S*___ how Chad Reed built his first sand castle

    b. ___*T*___ Chad Reed's experience building sand castles

    c. ___*G*___ making sand castles

2. Is your answer for the topic here the same as the one you determined after you previewed the text, or is your answer different? _____

3. What is the main idea of the text?

    a. ___*G*___ Making sand castles is an enjoyable way to spend time at the beach.

    b. ___*S*___ Chad Reed built his first sand castle ten years ago.

    c. ___*T*___ Chad Reed has been perfecting his sand castle building skills for ten years.

4. Is your answer for the main idea here the same as the one you determined after you previewed the text, or is your answer different? _____

B. Paragraphs. Write *T* for *Topic, G* for *Too General,* and *S* for *Too Specific.* Discuss your answers with a partner.

1. What is the topic of ¶2?

   a. ___T___ Reed's second summer of building sand castles

   b. ___S___ Reed's beach essentials

   c. ___G___ Reed's summer vacation

2. What is the main idea of ¶2?

   a. ___G___ Reed spent his summer vacation on Block Island.

   b. ___T___ Reed's second summer of building sand castles was somewhat more successful.

   c. ___S___ Reed brought some beach essentials: a pail, a shovel, and his experience.

3. What is the topic of ¶3?

   a. ___S___ Reed's green plastic beach pail

   b. ___T___ Reed's understanding the need for the right tools

   c. ___G___ tools for building sand castles

4. What is the main idea of ¶3?

   a. ___T___ Finally, Reed understood the importance of having the right tools for building large sand castles.

   b. ___S___ Reed brought a green plastic beach pail with him in his third year.

   c. ___G___ There are tools for building sand castles.

5. What is the topic of ¶4?

   a. ___T___ Reed's sand versions of major landmarks

   b. ___G___ Reed's sand castles

   c. ___S___ Reed's aqueducts

6. What is the main idea of ¶4?

   a. ___S___ Reed's aqueducts are a big crowd pleaser, and he tries to incorporate them when he can.

   b. ___T___ Reed reconstructs sand versions of major landmarks from around the world.

   c. ___G___ Reed builds sand castles.

6 | Understanding Subject and Object Pronouns

Write the subject or object that the pronoun refers to according to the text. Discuss your answers with a partner.

1. he (as fantastic as he had imagined) (¶1) __Chad Reed__

2. them (he tries to incorporate them) (¶4) __aqueducts__

3. him (Devin encouraged him) (¶4) __Chad Reed__

4. it (to use it when needed) (¶5) __water__

5. he (the sand castle he is making) (¶6) __Chad Reed__

6. I (I don't know) (¶6) _Chad Reed_

7. me (The sand tells me) (¶6) _Chad Reed._

8. him (helps him to relax) (¶7) _Chad Reed_

VOCABULARY STRATEGY Understanding Vocabulary in Context—Examples

Examples often explain unfamiliar words in a text. Examples are given with phrases like *for example*, *such as*, and *like*, or sometimes they follow a colon (:).

Read the following sentences.

1. Chad Reed made one of his first sand castles using only *the basics*: sand, his hands, and a desire to create. (¶1)

   What are *the basics*? The colon (:) that follows the phrase *the basics* indicates that *sand, his hands*, and *a desire to create* are examples of *the basics*. There are many tools someone can use to create something, but here he only used sand, hands, and desire. Therefore, we can guess that *the basics* is a phrase that means the most necessary part(s) of something.

2. Since then, Reed has reconstructed sand versions of major *landmarks* from around the world, such as the Eiffel Tower, Notre Dame, and the Hagia Sophia. (¶4)

   What are *landmarks*? The phrase *such as* indicates that the *Eiffel Tower, Notre Dame*, and the *Hagia Sophia* are examples of *landmarks*. We can guess that a *landmark* is a famous building or structure.

7 | Understanding Vocabulary in Context—Examples

Write examples from the text for each word or phrase. Discuss your answers with a partner.

1. beach essentials (¶2) _____

2. gadgets (¶3) _____

3. ancient Egyptian monuments (¶4) _____

8 | Discussing the Issues

Answer the questions and discuss your answers with a partner.

1. Chad Reed knows that his sand castles will be destroyed eventually, but he thinks that adds to the charm of making them. Do you agree? Why or why not?

2. Do you think that a sand castle is a work of art? Why or why not?

3. Would you enjoy spending hours at the beach building sand castles? Why or why not?

Text 2 | Ice Artists

1 | Getting Started

A. Answer the questions and briefly discuss your answers with a partner.

1. Have you ever been to a festival, fair, or carnival?

2. What festivals are famous in your country or region?

3. What kinds of competitions are popular during festivals and fairs?

B. Which of the following do artists normally create by carving or molding? Circle the letter of your answer.

a

b

2 | Active Previewing

Preview the magazine article on the next page. Underline the title, the first sentence of each paragraph, and the last sentence of the text as you preview. Then answer these questions with a partner.

1. What is the topic of this text?

2. What is the main idea of this text? (What is the most important thing the author wants you to know about the topic?)

3 | Reading and Recalling

A. Read the text. Stop after each paragraph and tell a partner two things that you remember about it.

White Heat

On Hokkaido, an island in Japan, the snow starts in November and doesn't melt until March. The solution is to celebrate.

BY WILL MARQUAND

Each February, Sapporo hosts Yuki Matsuri—the Snow Festival. As a result, over two million people flock to[1] Japan's north for this international event. They come to see the hundreds of ice <u>sculptures</u> and statues carved by ice artists—professionals, as well as amateurs[2], from all over the world.

2   Ice sculpting has become popular in recent years, but this festival is truly amazing because of its richness, variety, and splendor[3]. Majestic fairy-tale ice palaces stand several stories, or levels, high. Copies of famous <u>attractions</u> from around the world—Edo Castle in Japan, Angkor Wat in Cambodia, the Parthenon in Greece, and the British Museum in England—are <u>impressively</u> detailed. There are also giant Buddhas, dragons, and of course all kinds of cute characters, as well. The design, scope, and <u>complexity</u> of these sculptures and statues are <u>remarkable</u>, but they are destroyed after just seven days.

3   The festival occupies three venues, or locations. The heart of the festival is in Sapporo's downtown, Odori Park. During the festival, it holds more than 100 ice and snow creations. The nightlife district, Susukino, holds many of the crystal-ice statues that sparkle in the winter sun and night lights. Finally, there is the Makomanai Military Camp. Here are the most <u>dramatic</u> ice creations: enormous ice buildings, an ice karaoke bar, and a frozen playground where children can play.

4   The event's simple beginning was in 1950, when a small group of high school students decided to make snow sculptures in Odori Park. These first sculptures gave people heart and hope for a brighter future. Soon the local military forces were invited to participate. Consequently, a more formal event started to take shape. When they created the first truly huge snow sculptures, the festival took off: it gained fame and popularity very quickly. Because the military forces enjoyed the construction of the massive buildings so much, this task has become part of their training program.

5   In 1974, the Snow Festival occurred at the same time as the Sapporo Winter Olympics. With all the extra people in town, something special was called for. Therefore, a new competition was included in the festival: the International Snow Statue competition. Nowadays, teams from all over the world compete. Naturally, there are many competitors who come from colder countries, but there are also plenty of entrants from warmer climates, such as Hong Kong and Hawaii. There are also many contributions from public and private organizations, including schools and companies. Since the event attracts many spectators, the streets are lined with food stalls, and the statues are lit up at night.

6   There are two categories—the ice statues and the snow sculptures. "Ice statues" are creations that are formed from huge blocks of ice. The blocks are hauled to the venues by local trucking firms, and then the sculptors start to carve. Paint and lights add color, while a more exotic note is added by the use of live sea creatures, such as crab, squid, and fish, which are incorporated into icy aquariums.

7   The snow sculptures are created by a considerably[4] different process. "Snow sculptures" refer to creations that are carved from large amounts of tightly packed snow. Planning and design begin months in advance. A wooden frame approximates[5] the statue's final shape and is filled with

continued

---

[1] **to flock to:** to go to, in large numbers

[2] **amateur:** a person who does an activity as a hobby rather than a profession

[3] **splendor:** grand or wonderful appearance

[4] **considerable/-ly:** large in amount

[5] **to approximate:** to be or make almost the same as

continued

tightly packed snow. When the snow has hardened, the frame is removed. Builders use hatchets and shovels to outline the shape of the sculpture before they begin to carve the ice. They begin this work in the freezing night in order to avoid the heat of the sun.

8   The festival has now become an integral, or necessary, part of the Japanese winter. There is even complete coverage on Japanese TV, with regular broadcasts on the news and variety shows, because the festival has become so popular. In Japan's coldest corner, it is an event that brings great warmth.

B. Read the text again without pausing. Tell your partner two things that you remember.

C. Work as a class or in large groups. Try to name as many things as you can about the text.

4 | Understanding the Text

A. Answer as many questions as you can without looking at the text. Discuss your answers with a partner.

1. Where is the festival? _____

2. What kind of art is shown at the festival? _____

3. Where do people come from to see the festival? _____

B. Number the statements in chronological order according to the text. Mark the first event *1* and the last event *5*.

   ___2___ a. The local military forces were invited to participate in the Snow Festival.

   ___1___ b. A small group of high school students decided to make snow sculptures in Odori Park.

   ___5___ c. The festival has become an integral part of the Japanese winter.

   ___4___ d. The Snow Festival occurred at the same time as the Sapporo Winter Olympics, so the International Snow Statue competition was included in the festival.

   ___3___ e. A more formal event began to take shape.

5 | Understanding the Topic and Main Idea

A. Text. Write *T* for *Topic*, *G* for *Too General*, and *S* for *Too Specific*. Discuss your answers with a partner.

1. What is the topic of the text?

   a. ___T___ the Snow Festival in Sapporo

   b. ___G___ ice and snow sculpting

   c. ___S___ the beginnings of the Snow Festival in Sapporo

2. Is your answer for the topic here the same as the one you determined after you previewed the text, or is your answer different? _____

3. What is the main idea of the text?

a. __G__ Ice and snow sculpting are becoming more popular.

b. __S__ The beginnings of the Snow Festival in Sapporo go back to 1950, when a small group of students made snow sculptures in the park.

c. __T__ The annual Snow Festival in Sapporo is an international event that attracts many people because of its richness and variety.

4. Is your answer for the main idea here the same as the one you determined after you previewed the text, or is your answer different? _____

B. Paragraphs. Write *T* for *Topic*, *G* for *Too General*, and *S* for *Too Specific*. Discuss your answers with a partner.

1. What is the topic of ¶2?

a. __~~T~~ S__ ice copies of famous buildings and monuments

b. __~~G~~ T__ the amazing Sapporo Snow Festival

c. __G__ the popularity of ice sculpting

2. What is the main idea of ¶2?

a. __~~S~~ T__ The Sapporo Snow Festival is especially amazing because of the variety and splendor of the statues and sculptures.

b. __~~T~~ S__ At the festival, there are ice copies of famous statues and sculptures from around the world.

c. __G__ Ice sculpting has become more popular in recent years.

3. What is the topic of ¶3?

a. __G__ Sapporo

b. __T__ the locations of the festival

c. __S__ Odori Park

4. What is the main idea of ¶3?

a. __T ~~S~~__ Odori Park is the heart of the Sapporo festival.

b. __S T__ The festival is held in three different locations in Sapporo.

c. __G__ Sapporo hosts the festival.

5. What is the topic of ¶5?

a. __S__ the spectators attracted by the event

b. __G__ the Snow Festival

c. __T__ the International Snow Statue competition

6. What is the main idea of ¶5?

a. __G__ The Snow Festival is held in Sapporo.

b. __S__ The International Snow Statue competition began with the 1974 Winter Olympics and now attracts teams from all over the world.

c. __T__ The Snow Festival attracts many competitors from Hong Kong and Hawaii.

6 | Understanding Subject and Object Pronouns

Write the subject or object that the pronoun refers to according to the text. Discuss your answers with a partner.

1. They (They come to see) (¶1) _over two million people_
2. they (they are destroyed) (¶2) _Sculptures and statues_
3. it (it holds more than) (¶3) _~~festival~~ Odori Park._
4. they (When they created) (¶4) _local military forces_
5. it (it gained fame and popularity) (¶4) _the event (snow festival)._
6. they (before they begin to carve) (¶7) _builders_
7. They (They begin this work) (¶7) _builders._

7 | Understanding Vocabulary in Context

A. Examples. Write examples from the text for each word or phrase. Discuss your answers with a partner.

1. famous attractions (¶2) _Edo Castle, Angkor Wat, the Parthenon, the British Museum_

2. dramatic ice creations (¶3) _enormous ice buildings, an ice karaoke bar, and a frozen play ground_

3. warmer climates (¶5) _Hong Kong and Hawaii._

4. public and private organizations (¶5) _schools and companies_

5. sea creatures (¶6) _Crab, squid, and fish._

B. Synonyms and Definitions. Write the synonym or definition for each word or phrase according to the text. Briefly discuss your answers with a partner.

1. story (¶2) _level_

2. venue (¶3) _location)_

3. ice statue (¶6) _Creations that are formed from huge blocks of ice._

4. snow sculpture (¶7) _Creations that are carved from large amounts of thickly packed snow._

5. integral (¶8) _necessary._

Cause and effect relate to reasons and explanations for events, behavior, and conditions. The cause is the reason for an event, behavior, or condition; the cause happens or begins to happen first. An effect is what happens as a result of the reason, or cause.

To decide the cause of something, ask yourself *Why did this happen?* or *What made this happen?* Your answer is the cause. Words and phrases that show cause include, but are not limited to: *because, due to, since, for, one reason/cause is.*

To decide the effect of something, ask yourself *What happened because of this?* Your answer is the effect.

Words and phrases that show effect include, but are not limited to: *consequently, as a result, thus, therefore, resulted in, caused, one result is.*

Read the following sentences.

    cause ⟶ **effect**
1. Each February, Sapporo hosts Yuki Matsuri—the Snow Festival. As a result, over two million people flock to Japan's north for this international event. (¶1)

   The phrase *As a result* indicates that two million people coming to Sapporo is the effect of the event. Why do they come? The Snow Festival is the cause.

   Note: Sometimes the facts occur in a different order or sequence.

   effect ⟶ **cause**
2. Over two million people flock to Japan's north because of the Yuki Matsuri—the Snow Festival.

   The Snow Festival is still the cause and the two million people are still the effect even though their order is reversed in the sentence.

8 | Reading Critically—Cause and Effect

Read the sentences. Label the cause *C* and the effect *E*. Discuss your answers with a partner.

1. Soon the local military forces were invited to participate. Consequently, a more formal event started to take shape. (¶4)

   ___E___ a. The formal event started to take shape.

   ___C___ b. The local military forces were invited to participate.

2. Because the military forces enjoyed the construction of the massive buildings so much, this task has become part of their training program. (¶4)

   ___C___ a. The military forces enjoyed the construction of the massive buildings.

   ___E___ b. The task has become part of their training program.

3. With all the extra people in town, something special was called for. Therefore, a new competition was included in the festival: the International Snow Statue competition. (¶5)

   ___C___ a. Something special was called for.

   ___E___ b. A new competition was included in the festival.

4. Since the event attracts many spectators, the streets are lined with food stalls, and the statues are lit up at night. (¶5)

    C   a. The event attracts many spectators.

    E   b. The streets are lined with food stalls, and the statues are lit up at night.

5. There is even complete coverage on Japanese TV, with regular broadcasts on the news and variety shows, because the festival has become so popular. (¶8)

    E   a. There is complete coverage on Japanese TV, with regular broadcasts on the news and variety shows.

    C   b. The festival has become popular.

9 | Discussing the Issues

Answer the questions and discuss your answers with a partner.

1. Would you like to try carving ice statues or sculptures? Why or why not?

2. Would you travel a long distance to see an event like the Sapporo Ice Festival? Why or why not?

3. Do you think art should be competitive? Why or why not?

Text 3 | The Art Scene

1 | Getting Started

Answer the questions and briefly discuss your answers with a partner.

1. Have you ever visited an art museum?

2. What famous artists, if any, can you name?

3. What are some reasons why museums organize special exhibitions?

> **GRAPHICS** Previewing Tables
>
> **Tables** are used to present numerical or statistical information. **Preview** tables by reading the title, the column and/or row headings, and any **boldfaced** or *italicized* information.

2 | Active Previewing

Preview the table on the next page and then answer the questions. Discuss your answers with a partner.

1. What is the title of this table?

2. What are the four column headings?

   a. _____   b. _____   c. _____   d. _____

3. What is the topic of this table?

   a. the busiest art exhibitions   b. art exhibition attendance   c. art exhibitions

ART EXHIBITION ATTENDANCE

THE BUSIEST

Daily	Total	Exhibition	Venue
6,719	739,117	Van Gogh and Gauguin	Van Gogh Museum, Amsterdam
6,281	690,951	Van Gogh and Gauguin	Art Institute of Chicago
5,616	516,711	Masterpieces from the Prado Museum	National Museum of Western Art, Tokyo
4,671	467,166	Matisse/Picasso	Tate Modern, London
4,500	450,000	Surrealist Revolution	Centre Georges Pompidou, Paris
4,285	450,000	The Artists of the Pharaohs	Musée du Louvre, Paris
4,074	289,239	The Secret Gallery and the Nude	Museo del Prado, Madrid
4,052	218,801	Andy Warhol	Tate Modern, London
4,026	430,772	Treasures of Ancient Egypt	National Gallery of Art, Washington
4,020	333,695	Gerhard Richter	Museum of Modern Art, New York

THE EMPTIEST

779	82,594	Buddha: Radiant Awakening	Art Gallery of New South Wales, Sydney
779	101,216	Art from the Chicago Public Schools Collection	Art Institute of Chicago
777	76,919	Andreas Gursky	Museum of Contemporary Art, Chicago
776	38,000	Milan in a Van	Victoria and Albert Museum, London
770	43,149	Richard Artschwager	Serpentine Gallery, London
770	73,160	Impressionist Still-Life	Phillips Collection, Washington
770	81,643	New Architecture in LA and Douglas Gordon	Museum of Contemporary Art, Los Angeles
767	47,559	American Sublime	Pennsylvania Academy of the Fine Arts, Philadelphia
766	119,575	New York Renaissance from the Whitney Museum	Palazzo Reale, Milan
760	70,704	Treasures from the Kremlin	Indianapolis Museum of Art

3 | Scanning

Scan the table for the answers to the questions. Discuss your answers with a partner.

1. Which exhibition was the busiest? _Van Gogh and Gauguin in Amsterdam_

2. Which exhibition was the emptiest? _Milan in a Van_

3. How many people (in total) visited the Andy Warhol exhibition? _218,801._

4. Which exhibition appeared in the Victoria and Albert Museum in London? _Milan in a Van._

5. In which city is the Museum of Modern Art? _New York._

6. How many people visited the Matisse/Picasso exhibition daily? _4,671._

7. Which exhibition had 4,500 people visit it daily? _Surrealist Revolution_

8. Which venue held the Treasures of Ancient Egypt exhibition? _National Gallery of Art, Washington._

4 | Discussing the Issues

Answer the questions and discuss your answers with a partner.

1. Why are some art exhibitions busier than others?

2. What are some problems that could result from low attendance at an art exhibition?

3. Do you think it is important to visit art exhibitions? Why or why not?

Text 4 | Street Art Goes Inside

1 | Getting Started

A. Answer the questions and briefly discuss your answers with a partner.

1. Have you ever visited an art gallery?

2. Which of the objects or works in the photos are most likely to be sold in an art gallery?

3. Why do you think some people paint or draw on walls, as in photo *c*?

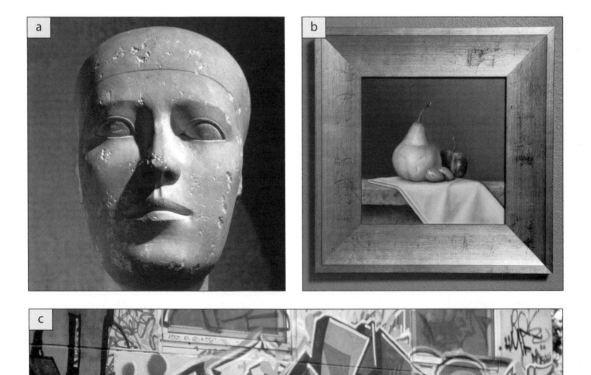

B. Check (✔) the statements that you agree with about graffiti. Discuss your answers with a partner.

Graffiti is ...
☐ 1. ... a form of art.
☐ 2. ... illegal to do.
☐ 3. ... something only children and teenagers do.
☐ 4. ... easy to do.
☐ 5. ... only done outside.

2 | Active Previewing

Preview the academic text below. Underline the title, the first sentence of each paragraph, and the last sentence of the text as you preview. Then answer the questions with a partner.

1. What is the topic of this text?

2. What is the main idea of this text?

3 | Reading and Recalling

A. Read the text. Stop after each paragraph and tell a partner two things that you remember about it.

From Graffiti to Galleries

Urban artist takes street art inside

1 **Graffiti or Art?**

Graffiti is often defined as illegal painting and drawing in public places. Doze Green, however, has a different opinion. Green is an artist, but his art is graffiti. Doze once used only public places—such as brick walls, freight trains, and alleys of New York—as his canvases. His artistry was not only unknown, it was illegal. Now, however, his pieces line art gallery walls from Milan to Manhattan, and corporations[1] commission his work. Green says this transition from street artist to gallery artist was unexpected: "Never in my wildest dreams did I think that painting subway trains ... would lead up to galleries and museum shows."

2 Green's real first name is Jeff, but he earned his nickname "Doze"—which means "to sleep"—in junior high because he used to fall asleep or daydream in class all the time. The nickname has stayed, Green says, because it represents who he is today. "I'm a dreamer ... I'm always in the dream state, so to speak, thinking about ideas."

continued

---

[1] **corporation:** a usually large business that exists as a separate legal entity from its owners or stockholders

3   Green's love for graffiti began in junior high school when his school sponsored a special graffiti event. Graffiti artists from Manhattan and the Upper West Side came down to do a mural. A mural is a painting that covers an entire wall or a large part of it, and Green thought it would be exciting to be part of such a big project. Therefore, he joined the contest. He did not win, but he says that the experience "sparked something" in him.

4 A Creative Outlet

When Green was growing up in the 1970s and 1980s, many of his classmates joined gangs. He says: "New York at the time was going through a serious recession[2]." According to Green, many kids joined gangs in order to feel like they were "part of something." But everyone knows that gangs can be dangerous and violent. People even get killed. Green believes that graffiti prevented him from getting into more serious offenses, such as fighting or stealing. "[Graffiti] got me on a more positive direction towards expressing myself instead of smashing a window or smashing a head," he says.

5   Eventually Green came in from the street and started painting in a studio in Brooklyn. One of his first attempts to make money from his art was designing corporate logos[3]. However, he eventually felt that the work became repetitive and didn't allow him to express his creativity. He began painting again. Gradually, more and more of his pieces appeared in galleries, and Green got more attention.

6 From the Street to Wall Street

Meanwhile, Green noticed that graffiti artists were not the only ones who were trying to reach people in urban areas. Advertisers wanted to reach a younger and more diverse audience and, as a result, were using some of the same methods he used. He began to see advertising on buses and trains. Green remembers that when he was still working on the

continued

---

[2] **recession:** a decline in the economy
[3] **logo:** an easily identified symbol used by companies or corporations

street, he and others would cover trains with tags and other graffiti, yet it was illegal. The new advertising technique copied their illegal art, but it was legal because corporations paid for it.

7   However, this new acceptance has opened doors for Green. For example, Green has created large murals on street walls for companies who want to reach a new market, including child, teen, and young adult shoppers—only now he gets paid for it. "It helps them; it helps us," he says. "It creates a great publicity for their image—youth-oriented. It's now. It's fresh."

8   While his corporate work earns him a good income, Green says it can also cause a bad reaction from fellow street artists if he does too much of it. Street artists believe that too much corporate work lessens, or decreases, the power and honesty of street graffiti. So Green is selective about the corporations he works for. "I won't work with certain corporations because of their practices overseas in manufacturing—certain clothing companies, certain soda companies."

9 Rawness[4] of a Street Artist

Green sometimes joins up with a disc jockey to create original works in front of a live audience. For Green, an audience can include potential clients, customers, or city residents. The practice, which he has been doing for ten years, reflects his roots—the foundation of his art. Before he became a successful artist, he was just interested in expressing himself though graffiti. "For me, it was almost like being a musician," Green says. He likes the pure spontaneity, or the total lack of planning. "Just a man, an audience, and his canvas alongside his music."

10   Through his corporate work and his gallery work, Green says he has been able to maintain his creativity. "I think I've retained that rawness," Green says. "That will always be there. That's not going to leave. What I'm doing, it's a new vocabulary ... new ways of looking at the same thing ... Whether it's accepted by the elite[5] or the guy in the street, what's important to me is people in general feel my work."

---

[4] **rawness:** freshness, originality

[5] **elite:** upper class; people with special privileges

B. Read the text again without pausing. Tell your partner two new things that you remember.

C. Work as a class or in large groups. Try to name as many things as you can about the text.

4 | Understanding the Text

A. Answer as many questions as you can without looking at the text. Discuss your answers with a partner.

1. What kind of art does Doze Green create?

Graffiti

2. When did he start creating his art?

In his junior high school year.

3. Doze Green's work is commissioned by _____ and also shown in _____ .

    a. small businesses, magazines

    b. film companies, movies

    (c.) corporations, galleries

B. Check (✔) the activities that Doze Green does or did that are mentioned in the text.

    ☑ **1.** shows his work from Milan to Manhattan.

    ☑ **2.** used to fall asleep in class

    ☐ **3.** joined a gang in the 1970s

    ☑ **4.** opened his own art gallery

    ☑ **5.** creates original work in front of a live audience

5 | Understanding the Topic and Main Idea

A. Text. Write *T* for *Topic*, *G* for *Too General*, and *S* for *Too Specific*. Discuss your answers with a partner.

1. What is the topic of the text?

    a. ___S___ how Doze Green became involved with graffiti

    b. ___T___ graffiti artist Doze Green

    c. ___G___ graffiti

2. Is your answer for the topic here the same as the one you determined after you previewed the text, or is your answer different? _____

3. What is the main idea of the text?

    a. ___T___ Graffiti artist Doze Green has made the transition from street artist to gallery artist.

    b. ___G___ Graffiti is a street art that many people pay attention to.

    c. ___S___ Doze Green became interested in painting graffiti because of an event sponsored by his junior high school.

4. Is your answer for the main idea here the same as the one you determined after you previewed the text, or is your answer different? _____

B. Paragraphs. Write *T* for *Topic*, *G* for *Too General*, and *S* for *Too Specific*. Discuss your answers with a partner.

1. What is the topic of ¶2?

    a. ___G___ how to get a nickname

    b. ___S___ Green's dream state

    c. ___T___ Green's nickname

2. What is the main idea of ¶2?

   a. _S_ _T_   Green's nickname, Doze, shows he is always in a dream state.

   b. _G_ _a_   Many people have nicknames.

   c. _T_ _y_   Green feels his nickname, Doze, represents who he is today.

3. What is the topic of ¶3?

   a. ___S___   graffiti artists who came to participate in the competition

   b. ___G___   graffiti contests

   c. ___T___   how Green became interested in graffiti

4. What is the main idea of ¶3?

   a. ___G___   Graffiti contests interest many graffiti artists.

   b. _T_ _y_   Green became interested in graffiti when his junior high school sponsored a special graffiti contest.

   c. _S_ _T_   Many graffiti artists came to participate in a contest at Green's school.

5. What is the topic of ¶8?

   a. _T_ _y_   how corporate work can reduce the power of street graffiti

   b. ___G___   graffiti

   c. _S_ _*_   Green's corporate work

6. What is the main idea of ¶8?

   a. _S_ _T_   Green is careful about the corporations he works for.

   b. _T_ _*_   Green says that many street artists believe that too much corporate work can decrease the power of street graffiti.

   c. ___G___   Graffiti is a popular art form.

6 | Understanding Subject and Object Pronouns

Write the subject or object that the pronoun refers to according to the text. Discuss your answers with a partner.

1. he (he earned his nickname) (¶2) _Green_

2. it (because it represents) (¶2) _nickname_

3. they (they were "part of something") (¶4) _~~gang~~ lords ._

4. him (graffiti prevented him) (¶4) _Green_

5. me ([Graffiti] got me) (¶4) _Green_

6. him (earns him a good income) (¶8) _Green_

7. it (it can also cause) (¶8) _corporate work ._

8. it (if he does too much of it) (¶8) _~~graffiti~~ ''_

7 | Understanding Vocabulary in Context

A. Examples. Write examples from the text for each word or phrase. Discuss your answers with a partner.

1. public places (¶1) _brick walls, freight trains, and alleys of New York_

2. serious offenses (¶4) _fighting or stealing_

3. a new market (¶7) _child, teen, and young adult shoppers_

B. Definitions. Write the definition for each word or phrase according to the text. Discuss your answers with a partner.

1. graffiti (¶1) _illegal painting and drawing in public places_

2. to doze (¶2) _to sleep_

3. mural (¶3) _a painting that covers an entire wall or a large part of it._

8 | Reading Critically—Cause and Effect

Read the sentences. Label the cause *C* and the effect *E*. Discuss your answers with a partner.

1. Green's real first name is Jeff, but he earned his nickname "Doze"—which means "to sleep"—in junior high because he used to fall asleep or daydream in class all the time. (¶2)

   ___E___ a. He earned the nickname "Doze."

   ___C___ b. He used to fall asleep or daydream in class.

2. Green thought it would be exciting to be part of such a big project. Therefore, he joined the contest. (¶3)

   ___C___ a. Green thought it would be exciting to be part of such a big project.

   ___E___ b. He joined the contest.

3. Advertisers wanted to reach a younger and more diverse audience and, as a result, were using some of the same methods he used. (¶6)

   ___C___ a. Advertisers wanted to reach a younger and more diverse audience.

   ___E___ b. They were using some of the same methods he used.

9 | Discussing the Issues

Answer the questions and discuss your answers with a partner.

1. Green says continuing his street art keeps his art "fresh." Why could this be true?

2. Do you think graffiti is a form of art? Why or why not?

3. Do you think it is a good idea for corporations to use graffiti in their advertisements? Why or why not?

Putting It On Paper

A. Write a paragraph on one of these topics.

1. Describe a style of art or a work of art that you like. Why do you like it?

2. Do you think art can be created only by trained artists or do you think that anyone can create art? Why?

Steps for your paragraph

a. In your first sentence, clearly state your opinion about the topic.

b. In your supporting sentences, use details to support your opinion.

B. Exchange paragraphs with a partner. First read your partner's paragraph and answer the questions in the checklist. Then give feedback to your partner.

✔ CHECKLIST
1. Does the first sentence clearly state the topic?
2. Are there enough details?
3. Do the sentences that follow give examples that support or illustrate the topic?
4. Is there any information in the paragraph that is not related to your partner's topic? If yes, please underline it on your partner's paper, and write it below:

_____

_____

_____

_____

_____

_____

_____

_____

_____

C. Revise your paragraph based on your partner's feedback.

Taking It Online | Art Smart

A. With a partner, use the Internet to research two artists.

1. Use Google (www.google.com) or another major search engine to find Websites with information about two of the following artists:

Andy Warhol	Marlene Dumas	Marc Chagall
Faik Hassan	Sawang Charoenpala	Vincent Van Gogh
Frida Kahlo	Tarsila do Amaral	

ONLINE TIP

Use the computer to help you scan pages by pressing CTRL+F and typing your search word in the box.

2. Preview the Websites as you would a magazine article.

B. Complete the tables with the information you find.

Artist:	*Claude Monet*
Website address:	*www.wikipedia.org*
Nationality:	*French*
Date of Birth: Date of Death (if applicable):	*November 14, 1840* *December 5, 1926*
Style of art:	*Impressionism*
One interesting fact about this artist:	*One of his paintings (Impression, Sunrise) was the reason for the term "impressionism."*

Artist:	
Website address:	
Nationality:	
Date of Birth:	Date of Death (if applicable):
Style of art:	
One interesting fact about this artist:	

Artist:	
Website address:	
Nationality:	
Date of Birth:	Date of Death (if applicable):
Style of art:	
One interesting fact about this artist:	

C. Following up. Post copies of paintings or pieces of art created by one of the artists you researched around the classroom. Tell your classmates about your artist's work and see if they can match your description with the correct painting or piece of art.

Redefining Activism

Answer the questions and briefly discuss your answers with a partner.

1. Do you play sports?

2. What sports are the athletes in the photos doing?

3. Do you think the people in the photos are typical athletes? Why or why not?

physically challenged.

fins.

Text 1 | Hold Your Breath

1 | Getting Started

A. Answer the questions and briefly discuss your answers with a partner.

1. Do you like to swim?

2. How long do you think you can hold your breath underwater?

3. Match the name of each activity with the correct photo.

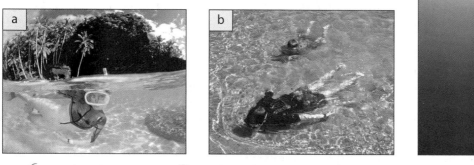

___C___ **1.** freediving   ___a___ **2.** snorkeling   ___b___ **3.** floating

B. Check (✔) all the things that you think are important for someone who likes to do water sports. Briefly discuss your answers with a partner.

A person who does water sports must ...	
☐ 1. ... be physically fit.	☐ 4. ... know a lot about the ocean.
☐ 2. ... love the ocean.	☐ 5. ... practice his or her sport often.
☐ 3. ... have a lot of money.	☐ 6. ... like to compete.

2 | Active Previewing

A. Preview the newspaper article on the next page by reading the first two paragraphs. Then answer the questions with a partner.

1. Who is this text about?

2. What does she do?

3. Where does she do it?

B. Answer these questions with a partner.

1. What is the topic of the text?

2. What is the main idea of the text?

3 | Reading and Recalling

A. Read the text. Stop after each paragraph and tell a partner two things that you remember about it.

Swimming with the Fishes

NO OXYGEN? NO PROBLEM. THIS FREEDIVER CAN STAY UNDERWATER FOR SIX MINUTES.

1   If someone told you she could hold her breath for six minutes, would you believe her? Tanya Streeter is a professional freediver. Unlike scuba divers, freedivers don't use oxygen tanks; freedivers dive while holding their breath. Streeter can stay underwater without oxygen for more than six minutes.

2   Streeter has broken nine world records for holding her breath underwater. She does it several ways: diving in the ocean, swimming in a pool, or floating. She can hold her breath longest when she floats, because she's not moving.

3   In 2005, she set a world record by swimming 374 feet (114 meters) underwater. (Imagine swimming almost five laps[1] in a swimming pool without taking a breath!) But an hour later a Russian swimmer swam even farther!

4   Streeter holds the record for diving into the ocean 525 feet (160 meters) below the surface. How far down is that? For comparison, the Washington Monument is 555 feet (169 meters) tall.

5   Freediving itself is an ancient activity, but the sport of freediving is relatively new. The first formal competitions started in the early 1990s. Now they are held all over the world.

6   Streeter loves the sport because it has taught her that it's almost always possible to do more than you think you can. When she first started freediving, for example, Streeter never thought she'd dive deeper than 100 feet (30.5 meters).

7   Streeter also uses her underwater efforts to call attention to the beauty and needs of the undersea world. She works with conservation groups[2] that help protect ocean life. "I have a very personal and almost spiritual bond with the ocean," she said.

8   Streeter was raised on the Cayman Islands in the Caribbean. Instead of a usual childhood, her childhood on the islands was unique. While most 7-year-old children spend their time with normal childhood pastimes—playing ball, playing games, and watching TV—Streeter was snorkeling in the ocean for hours at a time. "It never occurred to me[3] that kids anywhere else in the world weren't doing the same thing," she said.

9   When she was 24, Streeter began competing as a freediver. Today she is very well known. As a result, she now earns a living doing television shows and commercials. Companies also pay her to use their products.

10   Streeter is able to hold her breath so long in part because she's extremely fit. She's also helped by the way the human body reacts when it's immersed[4] in water, especially cold water. At first the heart beats faster; then it slows down, conserving oxygen by sending blood only to the brain and the vital organs, such as the heart, lungs, and liver. This biological effect is called the "dive reflex," and it is how marine mammals, including whales and dolphins, can spend long periods of time underwater.

11   A good freediver has to be mentally strong to fight the urge to come up for air. Since freediving can be dangerous, divers must take precautions[5]. For safety's sake, freedivers should always dive with a buddy as opposed to diving alone. Streeter knows kids love to see how long they can hold their breath, but she says no one should try to hold their breath underwater alone. "Even at my level of the sport—especially at my level—I absolutely, categorically, have a buddy," she said.

---

[1] **lap:** a complete circle around something; here, it refers to swimming two full lengths of a swimming pool

[2] **conservation group:** an organization that works to protect something, such as animals or the environment

[3] **to occur to someone:** to be understood by someone; to be clear to someone

[4] **to immerse:** to cover completely with something

[5] **to take precautions:** to plan for safety

B. Read the text again without pausing. Tell your partner two new things that you remember.

C. Work as a class or in large groups. Try to name as many things as you can about the text.

4 | Understanding the Text

A. Answer as many questions as you can without looking at the text. Discuss your answers with a partner.

1. What is Tanya Streeter's sport called? _Freediving_

2. What does Streeter do to break and set world records?
   Learn how the body works

3. What is one reason that Streeter loves her sport? _____
   She thinks the sports taught it's almost always possible than you think you can

B. Write _T_ for _True_ and _F_ for _False_ according to the text. Discuss your answers with a partner.

___F___ 1. Streeter has broken 12 world records for holding her breath underwater.

___T___ 2. The first formal freediving competitions started in the early 1990s.

___F___ 3. Streeter works with conservation groups that help to protect desert animals.

___F___ 4. When Streeter was a child, she did not enjoy snorkeling.

___T___ 5. Streeter now earns a living doing television shows and commercials.

5 | Understanding the Topic and Main Idea

Answer the questions and write _MI_ for _Main Idea_, _G_ for _Too General_, and _S_ for _Too Specific_. Discuss your answers with a partner.

1. What is the topic of the text?
   Streeter's freediving

2. Is your answer for the topic here the same as the one you determined after you previewed the text, or is your answer different? _____

3. What is the main idea?

   a. ___T___ Tanya Streeter is a professional freediver.

   b. ___S___ Tanya Streeter had an unusual childhood.

   c. _G S_ Freedivers dive in the ocean without using oxygen tanks.

4. Is your answer for the main idea here the same as the one you determined after you previewed the text, or is your answer different? _____

Another strategy for understanding unfamiliar words is to look for **contrasts**. Contrasts show differences between two words or phrases. Contrast indicators are words and phrases such as *unlike, as opposed to, not, but, instead of, whereas*.

Read the following sentence.

Unlike *scuba divers*, freedivers don't use oxygen tanks; freedivers dive while holding their breath. (¶1)

Who or what are *scuba divers?* The indicator *unlike* tells us that there is a contrast in this sentence. *Scuba divers* and *freedivers* are "unlike" each other. Why? Freedivers hold their breath while they dive, and they do not use oxygen tanks. Therefore, we can guess that scuba divers are divers who use oxygen tanks while they dive.

6 | Understanding Vocabulary in Context

A. Contrasts. Use contrasts to help you select the best definition for each word or phrase according to the text. Discuss your answers with a partner.

1. ancient (¶5)

   a. not new; very old

   b. relatively new

   c. the 1990s

2. unique (¶8)

   a. usual

   b. unusual

   c. similar

3. [do something] with a buddy (¶11)

   a. do it alone

   b. do it with a friend

   c. don't do it

B. Examples. Write examples from the text for each word or phrase. Discuss your answers with a partner.

1. childhood pastime (¶8) _playing ball, playing games, and watching TV_

2. vital organ (¶10) _heart, lungs and liver._

3. marine mammal (¶10) _whales and dolphines._

7 | Reading Critically—Cause and Effect

Read the sentences. Label the cause *C* and the effect *E*.

1. Streeter loves the sport because it has taught her that it's almost always possible to do more than you think you can. (¶6)

    _____E_____ a. Streeter loves the sport.

    _____C_____ b. It taught her that it's almost always possible to do more than you think you can.

2. Today she is very well known. As a result, she now earns a living doing television shows and commercials. (¶9)

    _____C_____ a. Today she is very well known.

    _____E_____ b. She now earns a living doing television shows and commercials.

3. Since freediving can be dangerous, divers must take precautions. (¶11)

    _____C_____ a. Freediving can be dangerous.

    _____E_____ b. Divers must take precautions.

8 | Discussing the Issues

Answer the questions and discuss your answers with a partner.

1. Have you ever tried or would you ever try freediving? What was it like, or what do you think it would be like?

2. Do you think that famous people should volunteer time with organizations such as conservation groups? Why or why not?

3. Do you think it is necessary to work hard at a sport or other activity that is important to you? Why or why not?

Text 2 | Rising to the Challenge

1 | Getting Started

A. Answer the questions and briefly discuss your answers with a partner.

1. Do you enjoy riding a bike?

2. Do you think it is important for people to play sports? Why or why not?

3. Where is Ghana?

    a. Asia   b. Africa   c. South America

B. Check (✔) the activities that can be done by people pictured in the photos.

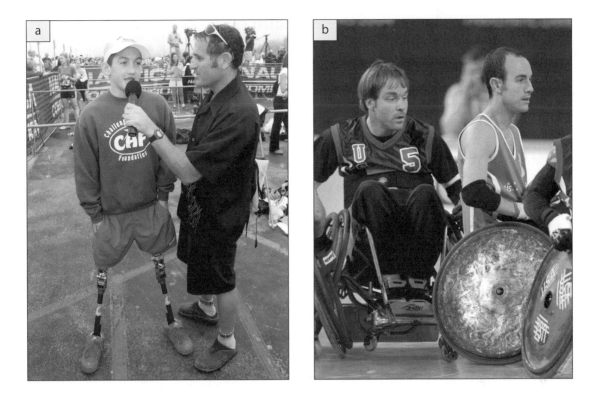

Activity	Photo *a*	Photo *b*
1. running	✓	☐
2. walking	✓	☐
3. riding a bike	✓	☐
4. playing rugby	✓	☐
5. playing soccer	✓	☐
6. playing basketball	☐	✓

2 | Active Previewing

Preview the magazine article on the next page. Underline the title, the first sentence of each paragraph, and the last sentence of the text as you preview. Then answer the questions with a partner.

1. What is the topic of this text?

2. What is the main idea of this text?

A. Read the text. Stop after each paragraph and tell a partner two things that you remember about it.

Ghanaian Helps Disabled Countrymen

1   Emmanuel Ofosu Yeboah was born in Ghana, his right leg seriously deformed[1]. This was not a great start in life for Emmanuel since in Ghana many disabled persons suffer great hardships, such as being hidden or unwanted by their families. In fact, the day he was born, his father—feeling shamed by his son's deformity—left the family.

2   Emmanuel's mother managed to send him to a private school, which was an advantage. However, she died when he was only 13, so Emmanuel had to leave school to earn about $2 a day shining shoes on the streets.

3   Disabled persons comprise about 10 percent of Ghana's estimated population, and Emmanuel began to dream of how he could inspire two million fellow disabled Ghanaians. He learned about the Challenged Athletes Foundation (CAF), based in Del Mar, California, which helps disabled athletes achieve their goals.

4   Emmanuel wrote to the organization, described his plan to attempt a 610-kilometer (380-mile) ride, and asked them for a bicycle. With support from CAF, he successfully completed his ride, wearing a shirt that read "The Pozo"—local slang for a disabled person. Throughout his journey, Emmanuel delivered his message of disability awareness, including the need for education for disabled children and the need for improved housing for disabled children who have no families.

5   Then CAF decided to fly Emmanuel to San Diego, California, to participate in CAF's Triathlon Challenge, a renowned athletic event that is a major fundraiser for the organization. After the event, CAF and Loma Linda University Orthopaedic & Rehabilitation Institute in California provided Emmanuel with an amputation[2] and an advanced prosthesis[3]. Last year, CAF again flew him to California to attend the Tenth Annual San Diego Triathlon Challenge, so that he could ride the 56 miles with his new prosthetic leg. Emmanuel was able to reduce his time from the previous year by more than three hours. As a result, he received an award, as well as a $25,000 grant[4].

6   Working together with CAF, Emmanuel plans to use this grant to pursue his mission of helping other disabled Ghanaians in a five-year plan. One of his first goals is to educate children with disabilities in Ghana each year. Emmanuel believes that education allows children not only to develop their minds but also to become involved in sports, thus empowering[5] them to do more than beg for money on the streets. Another of his responsibilities will be to oversee distribution of

continued

---

[1] **deformed:** not shaped normally, sometimes causing difficulty of movement

[2] **amputation:** removal of an arm or leg, or part of one

[3] **prosthesis:** an artificial body part

[4] **grant:** an amount of money given for a special purpose, usually by a government or foundation

[5] **to empower:** to give more personal power to

CAF sports wheelchairs to people with disabilities in Ghana. Lastly, he will direct the distribution of 250 everyday wheelchairs to people in need.

7　　Finally, a portion of the grant will be used to help Emmanuel with his own education. After his mother died, Emmanuel decided not to continue with his studies. Instead, he gave them up in order to support his brothers. He opened his shoeshine business and began planning his dream to ride his bike across Ghana and help others with disabilities.

8　　Emmanuel sees a great need for a Sports Academy for disabled persons in Ghana. Currently, there are two stadiums in Ghana. Able-bodied athletes can use these stadiums any time they want, but disabled athletes cannot. They must leave the facilities if able-bodied athletes arrive for training.

9　　The Disabled Sports Society of Ghana meets monthly to practice sports, but it has very little equipment. Often, disabled persons travel miles to attend, only to find there is not enough equipment for everyone. After a while, they become defeated and do not return.

10　　Emmanuel believes that by building the Sports Academy, disabled persons will have access to adapted sports, such as wheelchair basketball, wheelchair racing, and more. A chief of the Kibi region has offered land on which to build the center.

11　　Emmanuel believes the center will help Ghanaians with disabilities flourish instead of grow weaker. Emmanuel hopes that eventually, the help and training could even lead to a team from Ghana participating in the Paralympics.

B. Read the text again without pausing. Tell your partner two new things that you remember.

C. Work as a class or in large groups. Try to name as many things as you can about the text.

4 | Understanding the Text

A. Answer as many questions as you can without looking at the text. Discuss your answers with a partner.

1. What kind of physical disability does Emmanuel have? _Right leg seriously deformed._

2. Why did Emmanuel have to leave school? _To help children._

3. Whom does Emmanuel want to help? _The children in Ghana._

B, Complete the sentences according to the text.

1. Emmanuel's father _____.

   a. left the family after Emmanuel was born

   b. was very supportive of Emmanuel

2. The Challenged Athletes Foundation and Loma Linda University provided Emmanuel with

   _____.

   a. an advanced prosthesis

   b. a new sports wheelchair

3. Emmanuel believes in the need for _____ for disabled children.

   a. more money

   b. education

4. Emmanuel believes _____ can empower disabled persons.

   a. better nutrition

   (b). sports

5. Emmanuel wants to create _____ for disabled persons in Ghana.

   (a). a Sports Academy

   b. a learning center

5 | Understanding the Topic and Main Idea

A. Text. Write *T* for *Topic*, *G* for *Too General*, and *S* for *Too Specific*. Discuss your answers with a partner.

1. What is the topic of the text?

   a. __G__ bicycling for the disabled

   b. __S__ the importance of education for disabled people

   c. __T__ Emmanuel Ofosu Yeboah's efforts to help his disabled countrymen

2. Is your answer for the topic here the same as the one you determined after you previewed the text, or is your answer different? _____

3. What is the main idea of the text?

   a. __G__ Many disabled persons live in Ghana.

   b. __T__ Emmanuel Yeboah, a disabled Ghanaian, hopes to inspire other disabled persons in his country.

   c. __S__ Emmanuel Yeboah was born with his right leg seriously deformed.

4. Is your answer for the main idea here the same as the one you determined after you previewed the text, or is your answer different? _____

B. Paragraphs. Write *T* for *Topic*, *G* for *Too General*, and *S* for *Too Specific*. Discuss your answers with a partner.

1. What is the topic of ¶8?

   a. __S__ what disabled persons must do if able-bodied athletes arrive for training

   b. __S G__ the interest in sports in Ghana

   c. __T__ the need for a Sports Academy for disabled persons in Ghana

2. What is the topic of ¶9?

   a. __T__ the Disabled Sports Society in Ghana

   b. __S__ disabled persons who travel miles to practice sports

   c. __G__ disabled persons in Ghana

3. What is the topic of ¶**10**?

    a. __T__ building a Sports Academy for disabled persons in Ghana

    b. __G__ adapted sports

    c. __S__ a chief of the Kibi region

READING SKILL Understanding Supporting Details

A **supporting detail** supports or proves a main idea. Writers use details to develop their arguments. Supporting details can be **facts, opinions, data,** or **statistics**.

Reread ¶**6** on pages 96–97.

The main idea is: Emmanuel plans to use a grant to pursue his mission of helping other disabled Ghanaians with CAF in a five-year plan.

The supporting details are:

    a. one of his first goals is to educate children with disabilities

    b. he will oversee distribution of CAF sports wheelchairs

    c. he will direct the distribution of 250 everyday wheelchairs

The details all show how Emmanuel will pursue his mission of helping disabled Ghanaians through his five-year plan.

6 | Understanding the Main Idea and Supporting Details

Write *MI* for *Main Idea* and *SD* for *Supporting Detail*. Discuss your answers with a partner.

1. What is the main idea and one supporting detail of ¶**8**?

    a. __MI__ Emmanuel sees a great need for a disabled Sports Academy in Ghana.

    b. __SD__ People with disabilities who use facilities must leave if able-bodied athletes arrive for training.

2. What is the main idea and one supporting detail of ¶**9**?

    a. __SD__ Often, disabled persons travel miles only to discover that there is not enough equipment for everyone.

    b. __MI__ The Disabled Sports Society in Ghana does not have enough equipment for all the people who come to use it.

3. What is the main idea and one supporting detail of ¶**10**?

    a. __MI__ Emmanuel believes that building a Sports Academy for people with disabilities will give them access to disabled sports.

    b. __SD__ A chief of the Kibi region has offered land on which to build the center.

Possessive adjectives are like other adjectives in that they modify nouns or noun phrases. The possessive adjectives are **my**, **your**, **her**, **his**, **its**, **our**, and **their**. Possessive adjectives can refer to nouns or noun phrases that either precede or follow them.

Read the following sentence.

Emmanuel Ofosu Yeboah was born in Ghana, *his* right leg seriously deformed. (¶1)

Whose leg does *his* refer to? It refers to Emmanuel.

7 | Understanding Possessive Adjectives

Write what each possessive adjective refers to according to the text. Discuss your answers with a partner.

1. his (his father) (¶1) _Emmanuel_

2. his (his son's deformity) (¶1) _Emmanuel's father_

3. their (to achieve their goals) (¶3) _disabled athletes_

4. their (to develop their minds) (¶6) _children_

5. his (his own education) (¶7) _Emmanuel_

8 | Understanding Vocabulary in Context

A. **Contrasts.** Use contrasts to help you select the best definition for each word or phrase according to the text. Discuss your answers with a partner.

1. to give [something] up (¶7)

   a. to continue [doing something]

   b. to support

   (c.) to stop [doing something]

2. able-bodied (¶8)

   (a.) in normal physical health

   b. physically disabled

   c. athletic

3. to flourish (¶11)

   (a.) to do well

   b. to become weaker

   c. to help

B. **Examples.** Write examples from the text for each word or phrase. Briefly discuss your answers with a partner.

1. hardships (¶1) *being hidden or unwanted by their families*

2. disability awareness (¶4) *education and improved housing for disabled children.*

3. adapted sports (¶10) *wheelchair basketball, wheelchair racing, and none.*

9 | Reading Critically—Cause and Effect

Read the sentences. Label the cause *C* and the effect *E*. Discuss your answers with a partner.

1. However, [Emmanuel's mother] died when he was only 13, so Emmanuel had to leave school to earn about $2 a day shining shoes on the streets. (¶2)

   ___C___ a. Emmanuel's mother died.

   ___E___ b. Emmanuel had to leave school.

2. Emmanuel was able to reduce his time from the previous year by more than three hours. As a result, he received an award, as well as a $25,000 grant. (¶5)

   ___C___ a. Emmanuel reduced his time by more than three hours.

   ___E___ b. He received an award and a grant.

3. Last year, CAF again flew him to California to attend the Tenth Annual San Diego Triathlon Challenge, so that he could ride the 56 miles with his new prosthetic leg. (¶5)

   ___C___ a. CAF flew him to attend the Tenth Annual San Diego Triathlon Challenge.

   ___E___ b. He rode the 56 miles with his two functioning legs instead of one.

10 | Discussing the Issues

Answer the questions and discuss your answers with a partner.

1. Do you agree with Emmanuel Yeboah's belief that sports can help people develop more independence? Why or why not?

2. What is another way to draw public attention to a situation that needs to be changed?

3. Do you think the world is becoming more accepting or less accepting of people with disabilities? Why?

Text 3 | Good Sport

1 | Getting Started

Answer the questions and briefly discuss your answers with a partner.

1. Have you ever been to a large sporting event?

2. What famous large sports events can you name?

3. Pick one sporting event. What are some of the individual sports that are part of this event?

> **GRAPHICS** Understanding Schedules
>
> **Schedules** present a plan for an organized activity or event. **Preview** schedules by reading the title, the column and/or row headings, and any **boldfaced** or *italicized* information. Also preview any keys that help explain the schedule.

2 | Active Previewing

Preview the schedule on the next page and then answer the questions. Discuss your answers with a partner.

1. What is the title of this schedule? *Winter Olympics schedule.*

2. How much time is covered on this schedule? *16 days.*

3. What is the topic of this schedule? *the sports schedule.*

3 | Scanning

Scan the schedule for the answers to the questions. Discuss your answers with a partner.

1. When were the opening ceremonies? *Friday, February 10*

2. What does the symbol "⊞" mean? *final held in this sport on this day.*

3. How many days were there events in the luge? *5.*

4. Which events had finals on Day 16? *biathlon, cc skiing, curling, figure skating, ski jump, snowboarding, speed skating.*

5. Which event began on Day 8? *bobsled*

6. When did curling begin? *day 3*

7. Was there a snowboarding competition on Day 9? *no*

8. Which event had the most total days of competition? *ice hockey*

closing, cc-ski, ice hockey

Winter Olympics Schedule—Torino 2006

Winter Olympics Schedule—Torino 2006

February / Day	Fri 10 / 0	Sat 11 / 1	Sun 12 / 2	Mon 13 / 3	Tue 14 / 4	Wed 15 / 5	Thu 16 / 6	Fri 17 / 7	Sat 18 / 8	Sun 19 / 9	Mon 20 / 10	Tue 21 / 11	Wed 22 / 12	Thu 23 / 13	Fri 24 / 14	Sat 25 / 15	Sun 26 / 16
Opening/Closing Ceremonies	●																●
Alpine Skiing			❄		❄	❄		❄	❄	❄	❄		❄		❄	❄	
Biathlon		❄		❄	❄		❄		❄			❄		❄		❄	
Bobsled										❄	❄					❄	
Cross-Country Skiing			❄		❄		❄	❄	❄	❄			❄		❄		❄
Curling														❄	❄		
Figure Skating		●		❄			❄				❄		❄				
Freestyle Skiing		❄				❄							❄	❄			
Ice Hockey		●	●	●	●	●	●	●			❄				❄	❄	
Luge			❄		❄	❄											
Nordic Combined	●					❄		●				❄					
Short Track			❄			❄			❄				❄		❄		
Skeleton							❄	❄									
Ski Jumping	●		❄						❄		❄						
Snowboarding			❄	❄			❄	❄					❄	❄			
Speed Skating		❄	❄	❄	❄		❄		❄			❄	❄		❄	❄	

Key ● Event held in this sport on this day   ❄ Final held in this sport on this day

4 | Discussing the Issues

Answer the questions and discuss your answers with a partner.

1. Do you enjoy watching sporting events like the Olympics? Why or why not?

2. Why do you think some sports are more popular than others?

3. Do you think worldwide events like the Olympics improve relationships between countries? Why or why not?

Text 4 | Going the Distance

1 | Getting Started

A. Answer the questions and briefly discuss your answers with a partner.

1. Have you ever run, or would you be interested in running, a marathon?

2. Which athletic medal is for first place, second place, and third place?

_____ a. bronze

_____ b. gold

_____ c. silver

3. Is being a professional marathon runner a good job? Why or why not?

B. Check (✔) whether you agree or disagree with the statements. Briefly discuss your answers with a partner.

Statements	Agree	Disagree
1. Children should be punished for making trouble at school.	☐	☐
2. Children should study academic subjects rather than play sports.	☐	☐
3. Young people should have to work in order to pay for their university education.	☐	☐
4. Young people should choose professions or activities that they feel passion for.	☐	☐
5. Young people should choose professions that pay well.	☐	☐

2 | Active Previewing

Preview the academic text below. Underline the title, the first sentence of each paragraph, and the last sentence of the text as you preview. Then answer the questions with a partner.

1. What is the topic of this text?

2. What is the main idea of this text?

3 | Reading and Recalling

A. Read the text. Stop after each paragraph, and tell a partner two things you remember about it.

Taiwan's Marathon Man

1   It was Jan. 29, at the South Pole. The temperature was minus 29 degrees Fahrenheit (minus 34 degrees Celsius), and the wind was blowing at just over 60 miles (100 kilometers) per hour, with driving snow. A 150-mile (250-kilometer) super marathon[1] that crossed the South Pole had been interrupted by the snowstorm, and Taiwanese marathon runner Kevin Lin had a bad cold.

2   The race had begun two days before. The contestants ran 68 miles (110 kilometers) but then had to stop because of the storm. Lin was too tired and sick to guess when the race would start again, or whether the runners would be able to finish the event.

3   But by the end of the race, Lin had won the bronze medal. With that medal, Lin came in first place for four super-marathon competitions that had been held in far-flung locations: Antarctica, the Sahara Desert, Chile's Atacama Desert, and the Gobi Desert.

4   Last year, Lin came in second in the Sahara race. The year before, he won the seven-day, six-night Atacama ultra marathon, which crosses the desert known as the driest place on earth. He was the only runner from Taiwan to be invited to compete in the Atacama race. The year before that, Lin finished third in the Gobi March, and he finished twelfth in the Sahara race the previous year, after getting lost.

5   One month after Lin's athletic achievement at the bottom of the earth, president Chen Shui-bian gave him a special award.

continued

---

[1] **super marathon:** extra-long marathon, usually in difficult environmental conditions; also called an "ultra marathon"

6 From Punishment to Passion

Strangely, Lin's amazing achievements grew out of childhood punishment. Lin was known as a "troublemaker" when he was in elementary school. His teachers ran out of[2] ideas for how to punish him, so they told him to run around the school's track.

7   However, rather than being a punishment, running became a reward; Lin developed a passion for the sport. At the age of 16, Lin won his first official race, a victory that fixed his ambition to become an athlete. But Lin's parents opposed the idea because they thought he wouldn't earn fortune or fame[3] in a running career. Their disapproval made him decide to run away from home, although he didn't stay away for long.

8 A Helpful Coach

Lin's parents refused to support his desire to enter a "cram school" after he failed to pass the college entrance examination. As a result, he ran away from home again. He eventually returned home, but he decided to borrow NT$50,000 from his coach in order to enroll in the school. After a year of intensive study, Lin got his wish and entered the Taipei Physical Education College, where he majored in sports management.

9   In order to pay for his college studies, Lin worked odd jobs: as a gas station attendant, sushi bar waiter and pizza maker, and he even drove a taxi—earning NT$300 to NT$700 a day. During this time, Lin slept just three to four hours a day. Yet even with his busy schedule, instead of abandoning his training program, he continued to run four hours a day.

10   After graduating from college, Lin quit his jobs and studied for his graduate school examinations. But misfortune struck: he broke his right leg in a car accident and then failed the entrance exams. Even with these setbacks, however, Lin didn't give up. Instead, he persevered, and he finally got into the Graduate Institute of Sport and Leisure Education at National Chung Cheng University.

11   To support his passion for running, Lin wrote proposals and presented his idea of running super marathons to government agencies and private corporations. His proposal caught the interest of the Taipei City Government, the National Council on Physical Fitness and Sports, and China Motor Corp., which accepted his plan.

continued

---

[2] **to run out of [something]**: to have no more of [something]

[3] **fame**: public recognition; the state of being well known

continued

12 Bringing Attention to Taiwan

Wherever Lin goes, he carries Taiwan's national flag with him. He says he was inspired to do so many years ago by a top executive at a large soft-drink company. The man was also a serious runner.

13 "One day," says Lin, "I was at his apartment looking at his photographs. I was surprised that he posed with the national flag of Taiwan. … He loved Taiwan, even though he was an Englishman. I was born and raised here, so how can I not love this country?"

14 Lin's determination to carry a national flag became even stronger eight years ago when he was running a 62-mile (100-kilometer) marathon in France. Lin found out that the organizer had displayed his country's national flag upside down, but when he complained to the man about it, Lin was ignored.

15 "I suddenly realized that our country was like an orphan[4] in the international community. If the same thing had happened to the U.S. or the U.K., the organizer wouldn't have turned a blind eye to[5] their complaints," Lin said. "At that moment, I wanted to stand on the podium so much, so that the world would see where Taiwan is and how its national flag was supposed to be hung."

16 And the rest, as they say, is history.

---

[4] **orphan:** a child with no living parents; here, in reference to a country that lacks support or care
[5] **to turn a blind eye to:** to ignore

B. Read the text again without pausing. Tell your partner two new things that you remember.

C. Work as a class or in large groups. Try to name as many things as you can about the text.

4 | Understanding the Text

A. Answer as many questions as you can without looking at the text. Discuss your answers with a partner.

1. What does Kevin Lin do?

_____

2. Why did Kevin Lin start to run?

_____

3. Why is it so important for Lin to carry the Taiwanese flag with him?

_____

B. Circle the word or phrase in parentheses that best finishes each sentence.

1. Lin had a bad cold during the marathon at the (North Pole/South Pole).

2. Lin borrowed NT$50,000 from his (father/coach) to enter "cram school," so he could prepare for university.

3. Lin worked (odd jobs/at the university library) to pay for his college studies.

4. Lin continued to (talk with his coach/run four hours a day) even with his busy schedule at college.

5. Lin broke his leg and failed (the entrance exams to/his first term at) graduate school.

5 | Understanding the Topic, Main Idea, and Supporting Details

A. Text. Write *T* for *Topic,* *G* for *Too General,* and *S* for *Too Specific.* **Discuss your answers with a partner.**

1. What is the topic of the text?

   a. ___S___ how Kevin Lin began running

   b. ___T___ Kevin Lin's running career

   c. ___G___ Taiwan's athletes

2. Is your answer for the topic here the same as the one you determined after you previewed the text, or is your answer different? _____

3. What is the main idea of the text?

   a. ___S___ Super-marathon runner Kevin Lin developed his passion for running because of being punished by his teachers.

   b. ___G___ Super marathons cover extremely long distances in distant places and require a lot of training.

   c. ___T___ Super-marathon runner Kevin Lin had to overcome many obstacles to follow his desire.

4. Is your answer for the main idea here the same as the one you determined after you previewed the text, or is your answer different? _____

B. Paragraphs. Write *MI* for *Main Idea* and *SD* for *Supporting Detail.* **Discuss your answers with a partner.**

1. What is the main idea and one supporting detail for ¶10?

   a. __MI__ Lin broke his leg and failed his entrance exams.

   b. __SD__ Lin had to overcome difficulties in order to get into graduate school.

2. What is the main idea and one supporting detail for ¶11?

   a. __MI__ Lin's proposal to run super marathons was accepted by China Motor Corp.

   b. __SD__ Lin wrote proposals and presented his idea of running super marathons to government agencies and private corporations.

3. What is the main idea and one supporting detail for ¶14?

   a. __SD__ Lin was ignored by the organizer when he complained about how his country's flag was hung.

   b. __MI__ Lin's determination to carry the Taiwanese flag became even stronger when he saw that it was hung upside down at a marathon he ran in.

6 | Understanding Possessive Adjectives

Write what each possessive adjective refers to according to the text. Discuss your answers with a partner.

1. His (His teachers) (¶6) _Lin_
2. his (his ambition) (¶7) _Lin_
3. Their (Their disapproval) (¶7) _parents_
4. his (his apartment) (¶13) _Lin top executive_
5. its (its national flag) (¶15) _Taiwan._

7 | Understanding Vocabulary in Context

A. Contrasts. Use contrasts to help you select the best definition for each word or phrase according to the text. Discuss your answers with a partner.

1. punishment (¶7)

    a. penalty or harsh treatment for doing something wrong
    b. reward for doing something good
    c. a long and difficult race

2. to abandon (¶9)

    a. to give up
    b. to train
    c. to continue

3. to persevere (¶10)

    a. to continue, even when times are difficult
    b. to fail at everything
    c. to give up

B. Examples. Write examples from the text for each word or phrase. Discuss your answers with a partner.

1. far-flung locations (¶3) _Antarctica, the Sahara Desert, Chile's Atacama Desert, the Gobi Desert_
2. odd jobs (¶9) _a gas station attendant, sushi bar waiter, and pizza maker_

3. misfortune (¶10) _he broke his right leg in a car accident and then failed the entrance exams._

8 | Reading Critically—Cause and Effect

Read the sentences. Label the cause *C* and the effect *E*. Briefly discuss your answers with a partner.

1. [Lin's] teachers ran out of ideas for how to punish him, so they told him to run around the school's track. (¶6)

   _____ a. Lin's teachers ran out of ideas for how to punish him.

   _____ b. Lin's teachers told him to run around the school's track.

2. But Lin's parents opposed the idea because they thought he wouldn't earn fortune or fame in a running career. (¶7)

   _____ a. Lin's parents opposed the idea.

   _____ b. They thought he wouldn't earn fortune or fame in a running career.

3. Lin's parents refused to support his desire to enter a "cram school" after he failed to pass the college entrance examination. As a result, he ran away from home again. (¶8)

   _____ a. Lin ran away from home again.

   _____ b. Lin's parents refused to support his desire to enter a "cram school."

9 | Discussing the Issues

Answer the questions and discuss your answers with a partner.

1. In what ways do you think Lin has shown mental and physical strength?

2. What qualities are most important in order for someone to run super marathons?

3. How important is it to overcome obstacles or challenges in order to achieve one's goals?

Putting It On Paper

A. Write a paragraph on one of these topics.

1. Do you think practicing a sport for several hours a day is a good use of time? Why or why not?

2. Do you think that children should be encouraged to practice sports in addition to their regular education? Why or why not?

Steps for your paragraph

   a. In your first sentence, clearly state your opinion about the topic.

   b. In your supporting sentences, use details that support your opinion.

B. Exchange paragraphs with a partner. First, read your partner's paragraph and answer the questions in the checklist. Then give feedback to your partner.

✔ CHECKLIST
1. Does the first sentence clearly show which topic your partner chose?
2. Do the following sentences give examples that support or illustrate the topic?
3. Does the paragraph show clearly your partner's point of view about his or her topic?
4. Is there any information in the paragraph that is not related to your partner's topic? If yes, please underline it on your partner's paper, and write it below:

_____

_____

_____

_____

_____

_____

_____

_____

_____

C. Revise your paragraph based on your partner's feedback.

Taking It Online | Unusual Sports

A. With a partner, use the Internet to research two lesser known sports.

1. Use Google (www.google.com) or another major search engine to find Websites with information about two of the following sports:

archery	curling	croquet
bicycle observed trials	fencing	street luge

2. Preview the Websites.

ONLINE TIP

Information about a subject can differ from Website to Website. Consider reading more than one Website to get the most accurate information.

B. Complete the tables with the information you find.

Sport: snow ski jumping
Website address(es): http://en.wikipedia.org/wiki/Ski_jumping
Sport description: The skier goes down a hill with a take-off ramp at the bottom. He or she tries to "fly" as far as possible, but he or she also gets points for style.
Where was it invented? Norway   When was it invented? the 1860s
One interesting fact about this sport: Almost all world-class ski jumpers come from Scandinavia, Central Europe, or Japan.

Sport:
Website address(es):
Sport description:
Where was it invented?   When was it invented?
One interesting fact about this sport:

Sport:
Website address(es):
Sport description:
Where was it invented?   When was it invented?
One interesting fact about this sport:

C. Following up. Make a poster that presents one of the sports you researched. Include a brief history of the sport, a description, pictures, and illustrations. Hang the posters in the classroom for everyone to read.

Chapter 6

Marine Behavior

Answer the questions and briefly discuss your answers with a partner.

1. Have you ever seen any marine animals?

2. Look at the photos. What are these marine animals called?

3. What other marine animals can you name?

a

b

c

Text 1 | Danger in the Sea

1 | Getting Started

A. Answer the questions and briefly discuss your answers with a partner.

1. Have you ever been stung by an animal or insect?

2. What can happen if you are stung?

3. What are some animal and insect stings that can be deadly?

B. Look at the photos and fill in the chart on the next page.

Marine Animal	Photo	This animal stings.	This animal has tentacles.	This animal can be dangerous to humans.
1. octopus		☐	☐	☐
2. stingray		☐	☐	☐
3. fish		☐	☐	☐
4. jellyfish		☐	☐	☐
5. crab		☐	☐	☐

2 | Active Previewing

Preview the online article below. Underline the title, the first sentence of each paragraph, and the last sentence of the text as you preview. Then answer the questions with a partner.

1. What is the topic of this text?

2. What is the main idea of this text?

3 | Reading and Recalling

A. Read the text. Stop after each paragraph and tell a partner two things that you remember about it.

The Sea Wasp: Australia's Marine Killer

1 **Profile of a Spineless Killer**
From October to May, the North Queensland beaches are haunted by a deadly animal. These creatures belong to a group of animals related to the jellyfish. Scientists named them Cubozoans for their box-like shape. Local residents call them box jellyfish or stingers.

2 Box jellyfish have a square-shaped body with tentacles hanging down from the corners. All box jellies can sting using nematocysts, tiny stinging cells that cover their tentacles. When an animal touches the box jellyfish, the nematocysts release a venom that paralyzes[1] and kills the box jelly's prey.

3 While the venom of some box jellies is harmless to humans, the venom of others is extremely dangerous. An encounter with one type of box jellyfish—Australia's sea wasp

continued

---
[1] **to paralyze:** to make something unable to move

(*Chironex fleckeri*)—could be fatal. The sea wasp possesses the most potent venom of any marine creature. Therefore, even a slight brush of a mature sea wasp's tentacle against the body can cause heart failure and death within minutes.

4   At a glance, the sea wasp may appear like a jellyfish, but nothing could be further from the truth. Unlike true jellyfish, which depend on the wind and current to move them, all box jellyfish can swim. The sea wasp has been clocked at three knots, or 3.35 miles per hour.

5   The translucent[2] body of a sea wasp may grow to be as large as a basketball. Adults may have up to 15 of the stinging tentacles, three meters (nine feet) long, dangling from each corner of the sea wasp's body.

6   The animal even has eyes, three on each corner. "The animals have eyes but no brain. No one knows how they process[3] what they see," according to Jamie Seymour. Seymour is the leading researcher of box jellyfish at James Cook University's Tropical Australia Stinger Research Unit (TASRU) and has been studying these animals for 10 years.

7   **The Victims**
Seymour and his team are involved in a series of research projects because they want to understand these animals better. Some of his research is devoted to learning how and why the venom is so potent to humans.

8   "The venom is not targeted to humans," states Seymour. Instead, he explains that the sea wasp is a hunting fish. While most box jellyfish eat only invertebrates (animals without backbones), the venom of the sea wasp is targeted toward a vertebrate nervous system, like ours. The venom is also particularly potent. "Jellyfish don't have hands or feet," Seymour remarks. "They have to kill and kill instantly." The venom has a direct effect on the heart and, as a result, it causes immediate death to the tissue[4] it contacts.

9   **Treatment and Prevention**
It is important for the victim of a sea wasp sting to get treatment immediately, as death can occur in minutes. Twenty percent of the nematocysts fire when a person is stung. If the victim does not die right away, vinegar[5] can prevent the remaining stinging cells from injecting venom into the victim.

10   It is much better to avoid box jellyfish instead of meeting up with them. Seymour and his fellow researchers are becoming more accurate with predicting the beginning and the end of the box jellyfish season. During these months, swimmers, snorkelers, and scuba divers are encouraged to wear "stinger suits," full-body protective gear. Swimming is also allowed within nets that prevent sea wasps and other box jellies from entering the area. In time, the number of casualties from box jellyfish may be reduced to zero.

---

[2] **translucent:** partially clear

[3] **to process:** to understand

[4] **tissue:** here, a group of cells that work together to perform a specific function

[5] **vinegar:** a sour, acidic liquid used in cooking

B. Read the text again without pausing. Tell your partner two new things that you remember.

C. Work as a class or in large groups. Try to name as many things as you can about the text.

4 | Understanding the Text

A. Answer as many questions as you can without looking at the text. Discuss your answers with a partner.

1. What marine animal is described in the text? _____

2. How does this animal sting its prey? _____

3. If a person is stung by this animal, what could happen to him or her? _____

B. Check (✔) the statement that best describes the animal discussed in the text.

It ...
☐ 1. ... has a square, translucent body with long tentacles hanging down from the corners.
☐ 2. ... is a large, fast-swimming river fish with two eyes.
☐ 3. ... is a flying insect, similar to a wasp or bee, with three eyes.

5 | Understanding the Topic, Main Idea, and Supporting Details

A. Text. Answer the questions and write T for *Topic*, G for *Too General*, and S for *Too Specific*. Discuss your answers with a partner.

1. What is the topic of the text? _____

2. Is your answer for the topic here the same as the one you determined after you previewed the text, or is your answer different? _____

3. What is the main idea of the text?

　　a. _____ The sea wasp has long tentacles covered in nematocysts.

　　b. _____ The sea wasp is a very venomous marine animal.

　　c. _____ There are many venomous marine animals.

4. Is your answer for the main idea here the same as the one you determined after you previewed the text, or is your answer different? _____

B. Paragraphs. Answer the questions. Discuss your answers with a partner.

1. What is the topic of ¶3? _____

2. What is the topic of ¶9? _____

3. What is the topic of ¶10? _____

C. Paragraphs. Write *MI* for *Main Idea* and *SD* for *Supporting Detail*.

1. What is the main idea and which are supporting details of ¶3?

    a. _____ The sea wasp's venom is the most potent of any marine creature.

    b. _____ The venom of the sea wasp is dangerous to humans.

    c. _____ A brush of a mature sea wasp's tentacle can cause heart failure and death within minutes.

    d. _____ The sea wasp's venom could be fatal.

2. What is the main idea and which are supporting details of ¶9?

    a. _____ A victim of a sea wasp sting should get treatment immediately, as death can occur in minutes.

    b. _____ Twenty percent of the nematocysts fire when a person is stung.

    c. _____ Vinegar can prevent the remaining stinging cells from injecting venom into the victim.

3. What is the main idea and which are supporting details of ¶10?

    a. _____ There are many ways to avoid box jellyfish.

    b. _____ Swimmers, snorkelers, and scuba divers wear "stinger suits."

    c. _____ Swimming is allowed within nets that prevent box jellies from entering the area.

6 | Understanding Possessive Adjectives

Write what each possessive adjective refers to according to the text. Discuss your answers with a partner.

1. their (their box-like shape) (¶1) __These creatures_____

2. their (their tentacles) (¶2) _____

3. his (his team) (¶7) _____

Sometimes, we can understand the meaning of unfamiliar words by looking at the word(s) in the **context** of the sentences and paragraphs that surround them. To understand words through context clues:

1. Figure out the part of speech of the unfamiliar word(s).

2. Look at the surrounding information. See if this information contains clues about the meaning of the unfamiliar word(s).

3. Guess the meaning of the words using context clues to help you.

Read the following sentence.

In time, the number of *casualties* from box jellyfish may be reduced to zero. (¶10)

Who or what is a *casualty*? First, try to figure out the part of speech. The text is talking about a *number of* something, so *casualties* must be a noun. Next, look at the surrounding information. This paragraph talks about how people can protect themselves from box jellyfish, and this sentence discusses reducing something over time. We also know from the text that the main danger of box jellyfish is that they can sting and kill people. Therefore, we can guess that *casualties* means either *people who are killed by box jellyfish* or *stings.* We are left with two options. At this point, we have enough information to keep reading.

7 | Understanding Vocabulary in Context

A. Context Clues. Select the best meaning for each word or phrase according to the text. Discuss your answers with a partner.

1. venom (¶2)

   a. animal

   b. poison

   c. box jellyfish

2. prey (¶2)

   a. victim, animal that becomes food

   b. baby, child

   c. cell

3. fatal (¶3)

   a. deadly

   b. safe

   c. short

4. potent (¶3)

   a. comfortable

   b. powerful

   c. quick

5. brush (¶3)

   a. taste

   b. touch

   c. smell

B. Contrasts. Use contrasts to help you select the best definition for each word according to the text. Discuss your answers with a partner.

1. harmless (¶3)

   a. venomous

   b. not dangerous

   c. extremely dangerous

2. vertebrate (¶8)

   a. box jellyfish

   b. an animal with a backbone

   c. an animal without a backbone

3. to avoid (¶10)

   a. to stay away from [something]

   b. to enjoy

   c. to meet up with

8 | Reading Critically—Cause and Effect

Read the sentences. Label the cause *C* and the effect *E*. Briefly discuss your answers with a partner.

1. The sea wasp possesses the most potent venom of any marine creature. Therefore, a brush of a mature sea wasp's tentacle can cause heart failure and death within minutes. (¶3)

   __C__ a. The sea wasp possesses the most potent venom of any marine creature.

   __E__ b. A brush of a mature sea wasp's tentacle can cause heart failure and death within minutes.

2. Seymour and his team are involved in a series of research projects because they want to understand these animals better. (¶7)

   _____ a. Seymour and his team are involved in a series of research projects.

   _____ b. They want to understand these animals better.

3. The venom has a direct effect on the heart and, as a result, it causes immediate death to the tissue it contacts. (¶8)

   _____ a. The venom has a direct effect on the heart.

   _____ b. It causes immediate death to the tissue it contacts.

9 | Discussing the Issues

Answer the questions and discuss your answers with a partner.

1. Would you swim in an area where box jellyfish are found? Why or why not?

2. The text discusses ways that people can protect themselves from box jellyfish. What other ideas do you have for preventing box jellyfish stings?

3. Do you think that people should take time to learn about dangerous animals like the box jellyfish? Why or why not?

Text 2 | Male Competition

1 | Getting Started

A. Answer the questions and briefly discuss your answers with a partner.

1. Can animals be clever?

2. In the animal world, which males normally have the best chance of finding a mate—the big males or the small males?

3. Some marine animals disguise themselves by changing their appearance. What are some reasons for these disguises?

B. Match the photos to the marine animals listed below.

_____ **1.** shark

_____ **2.** cuttlefish

_____ **3.** starfish

2 | Active Previewing

Preview the magazine article on the next page. Underline the title, the first sentence of each paragraph, and the last sentence of the text as you preview. Then answer the questions with a partner.

1. What is the topic of this text?

2. What is the main idea of this text?

A. Read the text. Stop after each paragraph and tell a partner two things that you remember about it.

Fooled for Love

The male australian cuttlefish sometimes has to disguise himself as a female if he wants to get a date.

1 "The male cuttlefish has quite a challenge on his hands when it comes to the end of [his] yearly life cycle," explains Roger Hanlon, senior scientist at the Marine Biological Laboratory. "There are four, five, even ten males for every female on the spawning grounds. Therefore, the challenge each male cuttlefish faces is how to get its genes[1] into the next generation[2] of cuttlefish. Due to the low number of females, there is enormous competition among the males on the spawning grounds."

2 Rather than study fish close to home, Hanlon and his team spent five seasons observing cuttlefish underwater in a remote coastal area of Australia. As one might expect, the largest males used the advantage of their size to find a female partner and to guard[3] her from other males. However, Hanlon observed with interest that smaller males were able to get to the female while the guard male was fighting other males away, or by meeting the female in a "secret rendezvous[4]" under a rock.

3 Hanlon found that the small males with the biggest success rate use a special trick. They change their skin pattern and body shape to disguise themselves as females. Then they are able to swim right past a large guard male, who thinks he's getting another girlfriend. Hanlon explains that these smaller males do not try to fight the larger males because they must know instinctually that they cannot win.

4 While the larger males have a more direct approach, many of the smaller males use a sneaky approach, according to Hanlon. The small male cuttlefish will hide his fourth set of arms (females have only three sets), swell his arms up—as if he is carrying an egg—and change his skin coloration to a pattern that is usual in females. Then he just swims right past the large guard male. "And every single time that this happens," says Hanlon, "the big male looks and thinks he's acquiring another female mate and he lets 'him/her' just swim right in next to the female." Once the small male is next to the female, he can attempt a mating.

5 Hanlon reported in the journal *Nature* that although females rejected 70 percent of mating attempts overall, they accepted the majority[5] of advances from the mimics, or disguised males. The female cuttlefish collects sperm from several males. It is not until later that she uses some of it to fertilize her eggs. Hanlon also found that the females often used the mimics' sperm to fertilize their eggs. So mating in and of itself does not necessarily lead to fertilization. By using a genetic test called DNA fingerprinting, Hanlon found that the female more often than not fertilized her next egg with sperm from the mimic.

6 "[The female cuttlefish is] rejecting 70 percent of mating attempts, yet she's taking these small mimics at a much higher rate," Hanlon says. "Why is that? We don't know the answer, but there's something attractive, clever, some sign of fitness." He believes that perhaps the cleverness of the small mimic cuttlefish is an indirect sign of good genes in that animal. Therefore, the female will take the gamble of mating with him in the hope that he's a good match for her.

---

[1] **gene:** a basic biological unit that passes on characteristics from parent to child

[2] **generation:** here, the group of cuttlefish that will be born to the present group of cuttlefish

[3] **to guard:** to protect

[4] **rendezvous:** meeting

[5] **majority:** the greater number

B. Read the text again without pausing. Tell your partner two new things that you remember.

C. Work as a class or in large groups. Try to name as many things as you can about the text.

4 | Understanding the Text

A. Answer as many questions as you can without looking at the text. Discuss your answers with a partner.

1. Which male cuttlefish guard their females from the other males—the large males or the small males? _____

2. What do many of the small male cuttlefish do in order to get close to the females?

   _____

3. Which kind of male cuttlefish has the best success with females? _____

B. Check (✔) the correct descriptions according to the text.

This cuttlefish ...	Female	Larger male	"Mimic" male
1. ... uses size as an advantage.	☐	☐	☐
2. ... uses an indirect approach to mating.	☐	☐	☐
3. ... has three sets of arms.	☐	☐	☐
4. ... changes body shape.	☐	☐	☐
5. ... rejects 70% of mating attempts.	☐	☐	☐

5 | Understanding the Topic, Main Idea, and Supporting Details

A. Text. Answer the questions and write *MI* for *Main Idea*, *G* for *Too General*, and *S* for *Too Specific*. Discuss your answers with a partner.

1. What is the topic of the text? _____

2. Is your answer for the topic here the same as the one you determined after you previewed the text, or is your answer different? _____

3. What is the main idea of the text?

   a. _____ Female Australian cuttlefish reject 70 percent of mating attempts.

   b. _____ Australian cuttlefish have an interesting way of mating.

   c. _____ Smaller male Australian cuttlefish have better success with the females than the larger male cuttlefish do.

4. Is your answer for the main idea here the same as the one you determined after you previewed the text, or is your answer different? _____

B. Paragraphs. Answer the questions and discuss your answers with a partner.

1. What is the topic of ¶**1**? _____

2. What is the topic of ¶**3**? _____

3. What is the topic of ¶**4**? _____

C. Paragraphs. Answer the questions and write *MI* for *Main Idea* and *SD* for *Supporting Detail.*

1. What is the main idea and which are supporting details of ¶**1**?

   a. _____ Because there are more male Australian cuttlefish than females, the main challenge of the male is how to find a mate.

   b. _____ There are four, five, even ten males for every female cuttlefish on the spawning grounds.

   c. _____ There is enormous competition among the males on the spawning grounds.

2. What is the main idea and which are supporting details of ¶**3**?

   a. _____ The small male cuttlefish change their skin pattern and body shape to disguise themselves as females.

   b. _____ The small male cuttlefish are able to swim right past the large guard male, who thinks he's getting another girlfriend.

   c. _____ The small male cuttlefish with the biggest success rate use a special trick to get to the female.

   d. _____ The smaller male cuttlefish do not fight the larger males because they must know instinctually that they cannot win.

3. What is the main idea and which are supporting details of ¶**4**?

   a. _____ The small male cuttlefish hides his fourth set of arms and swells his arms up in order to disguise himself.

   b. _____ The large male cuttlefish thinks he is acquiring another mate and lets the disguised smaller male swim right by.

   c. _____ Once the smaller male is next to the female, he can attempt a mating.

   d. _____ The way the smaller male cuttlefish is able to approach the female is by disguising himself as another female.

6 | Understanding Possessive Adjectives

Write what each possessive adjective refers to according to the text. Discuss your answers with a partner.

1. its (how to get its genes) (¶**1**) _*each male cuttlefish*_____

2. their (the advantage of their size) (¶**2**) _____

3. their (They change their skin pattern) (¶**3**) _____

4. his (his fourth set of arms) (¶**4**) _____

5. her (to fertilize her eggs) (¶**5**) _____

7 | Understanding Vocabulary in Context

A. Context Clues. Match each word or phrase on the left with the best definition on the right according to the text. Discuss your answers with a partner.

_____ 1. challenge (¶1)   a. a risk; an act with an uncertain result

_____ 2. spawning grounds (¶1)   b. an act that fools or deceives someone

_____ 3. trick (¶3)   c. the act of starting reproduction

_____ 4. fertilization (¶5)   d. a test of one's abilities; something difficult

_____ 5. gamble (¶6)   e. a place where fish mate

B. Contrasts. Use contrasts to help you select the best definition for each word or phrase according to the text. Discuss your answers with a partner.

1. remote (¶2)

    a. underwater   b. nearby   c. far away

2. sneaky (¶4)

    a. indirect   b. small   c. direct

3. to reject (¶5)

    a. to accept   b. to attempt   c. to refuse

READING SKILL Reading Critically—Fact and Opinion

A **fact** is something that is true about a subject and can be tested or proven.

Read the following sentence.

There are four, five, even ten males for every female on the spawning grounds. (¶1)

Although the number of males to females varies, the fact that there are more males than females can be proven through documentation.

_____

An **opinion** is what someone thinks about a subject. Opinions may be based on facts, but they show a person's feelings about something and cannot be tested or proven.

Read the following sentence.

The male cuttlefish has quite a *challenge* on his hands when it comes to the end of [his] yearly life cycle. (¶1)

The word *challenge* cannot be tested or proven. We cannot measure objectively whether the male cuttlefish considers this situation challenging or not. It is only the speaker's opinion that this situation is challenging to the males.

8 | Reading Critically

A. Fact and Opinion. Write *F* for *Fact* and *O* for *Opinion*. Briefly discuss your answers with a partner.

_____ 1. The small male cuttlefish change their skin pattern and body shape. (¶3)

_____ 2. The guard male thinks he's getting another girlfriend. (¶3)

_____ 3. The smaller males use a sneaky approach. (¶4)

_____ 4. The female cuttlefish rejects 70 percent of mating attempts. (¶6)

_____ 5. The cleverness of the small mimic cuttlefish is an indirect sign of good genes. (¶6)

B. Cause and Effect. Read the sentences. Label the cause *C* and the effect *E*.

1. Due to the low number of females, there is enormous competition among the males on the spawning grounds. (¶1)

_____ a. There is a low number of females.

_____ b. There is enormous competition among the males on the spawning grounds.

2. Hanlon explains that these smaller males do not try to fight the larger males because they must know instinctually that they cannot win. (¶3)

_____ a. The smaller males do not try to fight the larger males.

_____ b. They must know instinctually that they cannot win.

3. He believes that perhaps the cleverness of the small mimic cuttlefish is an indirect sign of good genes in that animal. Therefore, the female will take the gamble of mating with him in the hope that he's a good match for her. (¶6)

_____ a. The cleverness of the small mimic cuttlefish is an indirect sign of good genes in that animal.

_____ b. The female will take the gamble of mating with him in the hope that he's a good match for her.

9 | Discussing the Issues

Answer the questions and discuss your answers with a partner.

1. Do you find it interesting to observe or read about the habits of unusual animals? Why or why not?

2. The largest male cuttlefish use their size to find a female partner. What are some other methods used by animals to find a mate?

3. What other animals do you know of that use size to find a mate?

Text 3 | The Ocean's Food Chain

1 | Getting Started

Match the animals with their prey.

Animal

_____ **1.** killer whale   _____ **2.** seal   _____ **3.** whale

Prey

a. shrimp   b. krill   c. penguin

GRAPHICS Previewing Diagrams

Diagrams give a visual idea of information. **Preview** diagrams by reading the title and any subtitles, and then looking at the diagram as a whole. If there are few words, read everything and focus on the content.

2 | Active Previewing

Preview the diagram on the next page and then answer the questions. Discuss your answers with a partner.

1. What is the title of this diagram?

2. What is the topic of this diagram?

3 | Scanning

Scan the diagram on the next page for the answers to the questions. Discuss your answers with a partner.

1. What is the top predator of this food web? __killer whale_____

2. What do seals eat? _____

3. What eats squid? _____

4. What do the primary consumers eat? _____

5. Do top predators eat primary consumers? _____

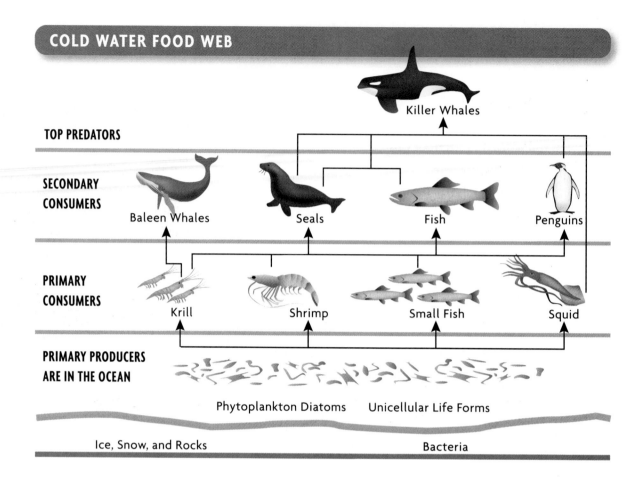

Killer Whales

TOP PREDATORS

SECONDARY
CONSUMERS

Baleen Whales   Seals   Fish   Penguins

PRIMARY
CONSUMERS

Krill   Shrimp   Small Fish   Squid

PRIMARY PRODUCERS
ARE IN THE OCEAN

Phytoplankton Diatoms   Unicellular Life Forms

Ice, Snow, and Rocks   Bacteria

4 | Understanding Vocabulary in Context—Context Clues

Select the best meaning for each word or phrase according to the diagram.

1. predator

    a. hunter; killer   b. shrimp or krill   c. cold water

2. consumer

    a. fish   b. animal   c. eater

3. phytoplankton

    a. large marine mammal   b. small marine organisms   c. aggressive killer

5 | Discussing the Issues

Answer the questions and discuss your answers with a partner.

1. What could happen to the animals in this food web if the phytoplankton and bacteria disappeared?

2. What could happen to the secondary consumers in this food web if there were an extremely large population of killer whales?

3. Why is it important to understand how food webs work?

Text 4 | Seahorse Fathers

1 | Getting Started

A. Answer the questions and briefly discuss your answers with a partner.

1. Have you ever seen the animal in the photo?

2. What is the animal in the photo called?

    a. sea urchin

    b. seahorse

    c. sea star

3. In the animal world, can males give birth?

B. Check (✔) the categories that apply to the animals.

This animal ...	... is a fish.	... lives in tropical waters.
1. shark	☐	☐
2. frog	☐	☐
3. seahorse	☐	☐
4. salmon	☐	☐
5. squid	☐	☐

2 | Active Previewing

Preview the academic text on the next page. Underline the title, the first sentence of each paragraph, and the last sentence of the text as you preview. Then answer the questions with a partner.

1. What is the topic of this text?

2. What is the main idea of this text?

3 | Reading and Recalling

A. Read the text. Stop after each paragraph and tell a partner two things that you remember about it.

Seahorse Fathers Take Reins[1] in Childbirth

1   It is true that male seahorses never play ball with their children or help them with their homework. But they do outdo human dads in one way: male seahorses go through pregnancy and give birth to their sons and daughters. This ability is unique to these strange and fascinating fish that live and reproduce in tropical and mild coastal waters worldwide.

2   Seahorses, which range from less than one inch up to a foot (from one to 30 centimeters) in length, have evolved a number of unusual adaptations[2]—a special tail that can hold on to underwater plants, a tubelike mouth for sucking in tiny sea animals, and protective bony plates in their skin. There are 32 species, or kinds, of seahorses, all belonging to the genus *Hippocampus.*

3   "They're such an unusual-looking fish, people sometimes don't realize they're real fish," said Alison Scarratt, in charge of fishes at the National Aquarium in Baltimore. Due to special bony plates that cover its body, the seahorse is unpalatable, or unpleasant to eat, to most predators. However, its survival is endangered by human predators, who hunt the seahorse especially for use in traditional medicines.

4   No statistical data on seahorse populations is available because relatively little research on seahorses has been done until recently. According to a network[3] of scientists from various institutions, fishers have reported a decrease in the number and size of seahorses they catch. These scientists conduct research under a program called Project Seahorse. The goal of this program is to find marine conservation solutions while using the seahorse as its main focus.

5   Although seahorses are easily able to breed[4] in their natural environment, breeding seahorses in captivity has been a problem, in part because the babies are so tiny that it is hard to keep them alive with the available feeding techniques. The marine scientists in Baltimore are working to develop effective methods that will help ensure the creature's survival.

6 Male Birth

    The male seahorse carries as many as 2,000 babies in a pouch on the outside of its stomach. A pregnancy lasts from 10 to 25 days, depending on the species.

7   The reproductive process begins when a male and a female seahorse do daily dances, intertwining their tails and swimming together. Eventually they engage in a true courtship[5] dance, which can last as long as eight hours. It ends with the female placing her eggs in the male's pouch. "Their mating ritual is quite beautiful," said Sarah Foster, a research biologist at McGill University in Montreal who is involved in Project Seahorse. Scientists think these movements have developed over time so that the male can receive the eggs when the female is ready to deposit them.

8   The eggs are then fertilized in the dad's pouch, and they also hatch in the pouch. The father cares for the young as they grow, controlling the water salinity, or saltiness, in the pouch to prepare them for life in the sea. When the tiny seahorses are ready to be born, the male expels the young from the pouch into the ocean.

9 Cutting the Ties

    While seahorse dads do more than most dads by giving birth, seahorse parents do not provide their tiny offspring (children) with any care or protection after they are born. Infant seahorses often die by being eaten by predators or by being carried away by ocean currents.

10   Fewer than five infant seahorses in every 1,000 survive to adulthood, which helps explain why so many babies are born at the same time, said James Anderson, manager of the seahorse

continued

---

[1] **to take the reins:** to take control

[2] **adaptation:** here, a change in a species that improves its ability to interact with its environment

[3] **network:** a group

[4] **to breed:** to reproduce, to have children

[5] **courtship:** preparation for mating

continued

program at the National Aquarium in Baltimore. Compared to other fish, however, seahorses have a fairly high survival rate. Whereas the eggs of other fish are abandoned immediately after fertilization, seahorses are cared for in the father's pouch during the earliest stages of development.

11 **Breeding Difficulties**

As far as seahorses' historical development is concerned, scientists are not sure what advantage male pregnancy gives them. One theory is that it takes them less time to reproduce since the process is shared by both partners. During the time that the male is preparing for the birth of the young, the female can prepare more eggs to implant in him soon after he has given birth to the last litter. Anderson said some seahorses can give birth in the morning and be pregnant again by evening.

12   Aquariums have only recently developed the technology to raise seahorses in captivity, according to Scarratt. It is extremely difficult because the infant seahorses are so small. While the adults are able to feed on plankton, the babies are incapable of eating organisms that are, for them, so large. Therefore, special food has to be grown so that they do not starve. According to Scarratt, the main challenge for the scientists is not getting the seahorses to breed, but helping the babies survive.

B. Read the text again without pausing. Tell your partner two new things that you remember.

C. Work as a class or in large groups. Try to name as many things as you can about the text.

4 | Understanding the Text

A. Answer as many questions as you can without looking at the text. Discuss your answers with a partner.

1. How do male seahorses differ from other fathers in the animal world?

_____

2. Where does the female seahorse deposit her eggs?

_____

3. What is the main difficulty when raising seahorses in captivity?

_____

B. Check (✔) the correct descriptions according to the text.

This seahorse ...	Female seahorse	Male seahorse	Both
1. ... has a special tail that can hold on to underwater plants.	☐	☐	☐
2. ... carries eggs in a pouch.	☐	☐	☐
3. ... places eggs in the pouch.	☐	☐	☐

4. … is hunted for use in traditional medicines.	☐	☐	☐
5. … controls the saltiness of the liquid in the pouch.	☐	☐	☐
6. … gives birth.	☐	☐	☐
7. … does not provide the babies with any care after they are born.	☐	☐	☐
8. … prepares the eggs.	☐	☐	☐

5 | Understanding the Topic, Main Idea, and Supporting Details

A. Text. Answer the questions and write *MI* for *Main Idea*, *G* for *Too General*, and *S* for *Too Specific*. Discuss your answers with a partner.

1. What is the topic of the text?

   _____

2. Is your answer for the topic here the same as the one you determined after you previewed the text, or is your answer different? _____

3. What is the main idea of the text?

   a. _____ Seahorses are very interesting animals.

   b. _____ With seahorses, it is the male who gives birth to the young.

   c. _____ Breeding seahorses in captivity is difficult because the babies are so tiny.

4. Is your answer for the main idea here the same as the one you determined after you previewed the text, or is your answer different? _____

B. Paragraphs. Answer the questions and discuss your answers with a partner.

1. What is the topic of ¶7? _____

2. What is the topic of ¶8? _____

3. What is the topic of ¶12? _____

C. Paragraphs. Write *MI* for *Main Idea* and *SD* for *Supporting Detail*.

1. What is the main idea and which are supporting details of ¶7?

   a. _____ Scientists think the seahorses' dance has developed so the male can receive the female's eggs.

   b. _____ The seahorses' true courtship dance can last as long as eight hours.

   c. _____ The seahorses' courtship dance ends with the female placing her eggs in the male's pouch.

   d. _____ The reproductive process begins when a male and a female seahorse do daily dances.

2. What is the main idea and which are supporting details of ¶8?

    a. _____ The eggs are fertilized in the seahorse dad's pouch.

    b. _____ The male seahorse cares for his young throughout pregnancy.

    c. _____ When baby seahorses are ready to be born, the father expels them from his pouch into the ocean.

    d. _____ The seahorse father controls the water salinity in the pouch.

3. What is the main idea and which are supporting details of ¶12?

    a. _____ Aquariums have only recently developed the technology to raise seahorses in captivity.

    b. _____ The main challenge for scientists is not getting the seahorses to breed, but helping the babies survive.

    c. _____ Baby seahorses cannot eat most of the plankton fed to adults.

6 | Understanding Possessive Adjectives

Write what each possessive adjective refers to according to the text. Discuss your answers with a partner.

1. their (play ball with their children) (¶1) __male seahorses__

2. their (help them with their homework) (¶1) _____

3. its (that cover its body) (¶3) _____

4. their (intertwining their tails) (¶7) _____

5. their (their tiny offspring) (¶9) _____

7 | Understanding Vocabulary in Context

A. Context Clues. Select the best meaning for each word or phrase according to the text. Briefly discuss your answers with a partner.

1. to outdo (¶1)

    a. to help

    b. to go through

    c. to do more than

2. to ensure (¶5)

    a. to make difficult

    b. to make sure

    c. to feed

3. pouch (¶6)

    a. sac or bag on the body

    b. pregnancy

    c. tube-like nose

4. to deposit (¶7)

    a. to dance

    b. to be ready

    c. to place or put

5. to expel (¶8)

    a. to prepare

    b. to force or push out

    c. to care for

6. offspring (¶9)

    a. children

    b. parents

    c. protection

7. infant (¶10)

   a. baby

   b. female

   c. fish

8. litter (¶11)

   a. unfertilized eggs

   b. historical development

   c. group of babies born at the same time

B. Contrasts. Use contrasts to help you select the best definition for each word or phrase according to the text. Discuss your answers with a partner.

1. in captivity (¶5)

   a. in a natural environment   b. in zoos or laboratories   c. underwater

2. to be abandoned (¶10)

   a. to be cared for   b. to be born   c. to be left alone

3. to be incapable of (¶12)

   a. to feed upon   b. to be unable to   c. to be able to

8 | Reading Critically—Cause and Effect

Read the sentences. Label the cause *C* and the effect *E*. Briefly discuss your answers with a partner.

1. Due to special bony plates that cover its body, the seahorse is unpalatable, or unpleasant to eat, to most predators. (¶3)

   __C__ a. Special bony plates cover the seahorse's body.

   __E__ b. The seahorse is unpalatable to predators.

2. No statistical data on seahorse populations is available because relatively little research on seahorses has been done until recently. (¶4)

   _____ a. No statistical data on seahorse populations is available.

   _____ b. Relatively little research on seahorses has been done until recently.

3. Scientists think these movements have developed over time so that the male can receive the eggs when the female is ready to deposit them. (¶7)

   _____ a. Scientists think these movements have developed over time.

   _____ b. The male can receive the eggs when the female is ready to deposit them.

9 | Discussing the Issues

Answer the questions and discuss your answers with a partner.

1. What are some of the benefits of raising seahorses in captivity?

2. Is it important for seahorses to survive? Why or why not?

3. Scientists aren't sure what advantage male pregnancy gives the seahorse, although they do have some ideas. What theories do you have?

Putting It On Paper

A. Write a paragraph on one of these topics.

1. What could happen if some ocean species disappear?

2. How can research on marine animals affect the survival of a species?

Steps for your paragraph

   a. In your first sentence, clearly state your opinion about the topic.

   b. In your supporting sentences, use details that support your opinion.

   c. Be sure to include at least one cause and one effect in your paragraph.

B. Exchange paragraphs with a partner. First, read your partner's paragraph and answer the questions in the checklist. Then give feedback to your partner.

✔ CHECKLIST
1. Does the first sentence clearly show which topic your partner chose?
2. Do the following sentences give examples that support or illustrate the topic?
3. Does the paragraph show clearly your partner's point of view about his or her topic?
4. Does the paragraph contain at least one cause and one effect?
5. Is there any information in the paragraph that is not related to your partner's topic? If yes, please underline it on your partner's paper, and write it below:

_____

_____

_____

_____

_____

_____

_____

_____

_____

C. Revise your paragraph based on your partner's feedback.

Taking It Online | Ocean Life

A. With a partner, use the Internet to research two marine animals.

1. Use Google (www.google.com) or another major search engine to find Websites with information about two of the following marine animals:

bottlenose dolphin	humpback whale	octopus
giant clam	moray eel	sea turtle

2. Preview the Websites.

ONLINE TIP

Use quotation marks in the search box to search for word groups or phrases:
"moray eel"
"octopus fact"
"sea turtles eat"

B. Complete the tables with the information you find.

Marine animal: sea otter
Website address(es): http://www.enchantedlearning.com
Where are they found? Pacific Ocean coasts, bays, and kelp beds
What do they eat? crabs, clams, mussels, octopuses, squid, sea urchins, fish, etc.
What predators do they have (if any)? some sharks and birds
One interesting fact about this animal: They don't have any fat to keep them warm. Instead, they have the densest fur of all mammals.

Marine animal:
Website address(es):
Where are they found?
What do they eat?
What predators do they have (if any)?
One interesting fact about this animal:

Marine animal:
Website address(es):
Where are they found?
What do they eat?
What predators do they have (if any)?
One interesting fact about this animal:

C. Following up. Draw a food web for one of your marine animals. Compare it with the food web of a classmate who researched the same animal. Are your food webs similar?

Medical Technology

Answer the questions and briefly discuss your answers with a partner.

1. Have you ever studied science?

2. Look at the photos. What does each one show?

3. How are ancient science and medicine important for modern science and medicine?

Text 1 | Modern Dinosaurs?

1 | Getting Started

A. Answer the questions and briefly discuss your answers with a partner.

1. Are dinosaurs alive today?

2. What modern animals are related to dinosaurs?

    a. crocodiles

    b. birds

    c. frogs

3. The art below shows a strand of DNA. What does DNA carry?

    a. personality traits (shyness, adventurousness, etc.)

    b. genetic information (eye color, height, etc.)

    c. preferences (favorite food, favorite color, etc.)

B. Look at the photos and fill in the table on the next page.

Animal	Photo	Extinct
1. Tyrannosaurus Rex (T-rex)		☐
2. ostrich		☐
3. desert bighorn sheep		☐
4. woolly mammoth		☐
5. horseshoe crab		☐

2 | Active Previewing

A. Preview the newspaper article on the next page by reading the first two paragraphs. Then answer the questions with a partner.

1. Who is doing research?

2. What did they find?

3. Where was it found?

4. When did they find it?

B. Answer these questions with a partner.

1. What is the topic of this text?

2. What is the main idea of this text?

3 | Reading and Recalling

A. Read the text. Stop after each paragraph and tell a partner two things that you remember about it.

T-Rex Could Bring *Jurassic Park* to Life

SCIENTISTS SAY DINOSAUR CLONING[1] POSSIBLE FROM DNA

BY DAVID ADAM

1   Scientists have raised the idea of a "Jurassic Park" rebirth of dinosaurs after extracting, or removing, what looks like blood vessels[2] and intact (undamaged) cells from a Tyrannosaurus rex.

2   The well preserved fossil skeleton of the T-rex that scientists are researching was unearthed in 2003 from Hell Creek, Montana, in the U.S. When the researchers analyzed one of its thigh bones, broken during its recovery, they found a flexible, stretchy material with what appeared to be transparent and hollow blood vessels inside it. The vessels branched like real blood vessels, and some held cell-like structures. Mary Schweitzer, from North Carolina State University in Raleigh, who led the team, told the journal *Science*: "It was totally shocking. I didn't believe it until we'd done it 17 times."

3   Tests on the 70-million-year-old samples continue, but the U.S. scientists have not ruled out the possibility of extracting DNA. The extraction of DNA was the starting point for the cloning of dinosaurs in Michael Crichton's bestseller "Jurassic Park," which was the basis for Steven Spielberg's hit film of the same name.

4   The blood vessels were similar to the blood vessels of modern-day birds. In appearance, they closely resembled the vessels from the bones of present-day ostriches, the scientists said. Many of these blood vessels contained red and brown structures that looked like cells. Within these cell-like structures, the team discovered smaller objects similar in size to the nuclei[3] of blood cells in modern birds.

5   Their next step is to examine the soft tissue found inside the bone; it might be original T-rex material. However, it could be that the proteins[4] from the original T-rex have been replaced by other chemicals over the centuries. Scientists have previously recovered intact cells trapped in 225-million-year-old amber, only to find the nuclei had been replaced with other substances over the years.

6   Dr Schweitzer's group said they had identified some protein fragments that still responded to tests.

7   Other experts were hopeful. In the UK, David Martill, a biochemist at the University of Portsmouth, said: "There's a reasonable chance that there may be intact proteins." He speculated that it might even be possible to extract DNA, but no one knows for sure whether it will be possible.

8   Lawrence Witmer, a paleontologist at Ohio University's college of osteopathic medicine, agreed: "If we have tissues that are not fossilized, then we can potentially extract DNA. It's very exciting."

9   If the cells do contain original biological material, the scientists would be able to investigate everything from dinosaur physiology to how the creatures evolved into birds.

10   Cloning a T-rex would be far more difficult. Current techniques need hundreds of nuclei from living cells, said Duane Kraemer, a cloning expert at Texas A&M University, who leads a project called Noah's Ark, which stores tissue samples from animals facing extinction, such as pandas and the desert bighorn sheep. Any dinosaur DNA remaining in the cells would probably be damaged or degraded, making it impossible to use for cloning.

continued

---

[1] **to clone:** to create an organism from the cells or DNA of a single individual organism

[2] **blood vessel:** a tube through which the blood circulates in the body

[3] **nucleus:** a part of the cell containing DNA and RNA and responsible for growth and reproduction (plural: nuclei)

[4] **protein:** a material that makes up most body tissue

continued

11   In the fictional Jurassic Park, scientists repaired damage using amphibian[5] DNA. In reality, they would need to know the complete dinosaur genome. "To determine what has been damaged you need to know what the original DNA sequence was," said Dr. Kraemer.

12   Alex Greenwood is a molecular biologist at the American Museum of Natural History in New York. He has compared trying to clone an extinct animal from damaged DNA to throwing all the parts needed to make a car down the stairs of a building in the hope of creating a Porsche 911.

13   This fact has not stopped people from trying to clone extinct animals. Several groups have made unsuccessful attempts to resurrect the woolly mammoth using genetic material recovered from a preserved carcass. For now, however, the technology to clone extinct animals successfully does not exist.

---

[5] **amphibian:** a class of animals that live half in the water and half on land, such as frogs

B. Read the text again without pausing. Tell your partner two new things that you remember.

C. Work as a class or in large groups. Try to name as many things as you can about the text.

4 | Understanding the Text

A. Answer as many questions as you can without looking at the text. Discuss your answers with a partner.

1. What did scientists find? _____

2. What was inside the bones? _____

3. Why are scientists interested in this discovery?
_____

B. Check (✔) the correct answers according to the text. Discuss your answers with a partner.

This event ...	... has already happened.	... has not happened (yet).
1. Scientists find a 70-million-year-old T-rex skeleton.	☐	☐
2. Scientists extract DNA from a T-rex fossil.	☐	☐
3. Scientists find proteins in the soft tissue of a T-rex skeleton bone.	☐	☐
4. Scientists analyze all the soft material in the T-rex sample.	☐	☐
5. Scientists clone extinct animals.	☐	☐

5 | Understanding the Topic, Main Idea, and Supporting Details

A. Text. Answer the questions. Discuss your answers with a partner.

1. What is the topic of the text? _____

2. What is the main idea of the text? _____

3. Are your answers for the topic and main idea here the same as the ones
   you determined after you previewed the text, or are your answers different?

   _____

B. Paragraphs. Write *MI* for *Main Idea* and *SD* for *Supporting Detail*. Discuss your answers with
a partner.

1. What is the topic of ¶4? _____

2. What is the main idea and which are supporting details of ¶4?

   a. _____ The blood vessels were similar to the blood vessels of modern-day birds.

   b. _____ In appearance, the blood vessels most closely resembled the blood vessels of present-day ostriches.

   c. _____ Within these cell-like structures, the team discovered smaller objects similar in
   size to the nuclei of blood cells in modern birds.

3. What is the topic of ¶5? _____

4. What is the main idea and which are supporting details of ¶5?

   a. _____ The soft tissue found inside the bone might be original T-rex material.

   b. _____ It could be that the proteins from the original T-rex have been replaced by other
   chemicals over the centuries.

   c. _____ Scientists want to examine the soft tissue found inside the bone.

   d. _____ Scientists previously recovered intact cells trapped in 225-million-year-old amber,
   only to find that the nuclei had been replaced with other substances over
   the years.

5. What is the topic of ¶10? _____

6. What is the main idea and which are supporting details of ¶10?

   a. _____ Current techniques need hundreds of nuclei from living cells.

   b. _____ Scientists say that it would be very difficult to clone dinosaurs.

   c. _____ Dinosaur DNA remaining in the cells would probably be damaged or degraded.

Collocations are groups of words that frequently occur together and are often idiomatic. Common collocation patterns include *adjective-noun, adverb-adjective,* and *adverb-verb.*

Read the following sentence.

In appearance, [the dinosaur's blood vessels] closely resembled the vessels from the bones of present-day ostriches ... (¶4)

This sentence contains two collocations. The first is an adverb-verb collocation: *closely resembled.* The second is an adjective-noun collocation: *present-day. Closely* means nearly. *Resembled* means to have a similar appearance. The collocation *closely resembled* means *a very similar appearance. Present* as an adjective means *current* or *today. Day* is a period of time. The collocation *present-day* means *today.* Recognizing these collocations helps us understand that this sentence means that the dinosaur's blood vessels have a very similar appearance to the blood vessels of today's ostriches.

6 | Understanding Vocabulary in Context

A. Collocations. Complete the chart and then fill in the blanks. Discuss your answers with a partner.

1. Write the correct noun next to each adjective. Then match each collocation with its definition.

Adjective		Noun	Definition
__c__ 1. hit _film_		chance	a. all body tissue except bone
_____ 2. modern _____		day	b. beginning
_____ 3. reasonable _____		film	c. popular film
_____ 4. soft _____		point	d. today
_____ 5. starting _____		tissue	e. very good possibility

2. Fill in the blanks with the correct collocation from the chart.

   a. The extraction of DNA was the _____ for the cloning of dinosaurs in Michael Crichton's bestseller "Jurassic Park," which was the basis for Steven Spielberg's _____ of the same name.

   b. The blood vessels [from the T-rex bones] were similar to the blood vessels of _____ birds.

c. Their next step is to examine the _____ found inside the bone; it might be original T-rex material.

d. "There's a _____ that there may be intact proteins."

B. **Context Clues.** Select the best meaning for each word or phrase according to the text. Discuss your answers with a partner.

1. to speculate (¶7)

   a. to guess or to think   b. to know for sure   c. to extract DNA

2. degraded (¶10)

   a. perfect   b. in bad condition   c. very new

3. carcass (¶13)

   a. living animal   b. people   c. dead body of an animal

7 | Reading Critically—Fact and Opinion

Write *F* for *Fact* and *O* for *Opinion*. Discuss your answers with a partner.

___F___ 1. The vessels branched like real blood vessels, and some held cell-like structures. (¶2)

_____ 2. Scientists have previously recovered intact cells trapped in 225-million-year-old amber. (¶5)

_____ 3. There's a reasonable chance that there may be intact proteins. (¶7)

_____ 4. Cloning a T-rex would be far more difficult. (¶10)

_____ 5. Alex Greenwood is a molecular biologist at the American Museum of Natural History in New York. (¶12)

8 | Discussing the Issues

Answer the questions and discuss your answers with a partner.

1. Do you think scientists will ever successfully clone extinct animals? Why or why not?

2. Should scientists try to clone dinosaurs? Why or why not?

3. Imagine that it is possible to clone extinct animals. Which animal, if any, would you choose to clone? Why?

Text 2 | Printing Organs

1 | Getting Started

A. Answer the questions and briefly discuss your answers with a partner.

1. Do you think the human body is simple or complex?

2. Is modern technology important for saving lives?

3. Which of the following organs do you think can be transplanted?

   a. blood vessels   b. bone   c. brain   d. heart   e. lung

B. Check (✔) the medical procedures that are used today.

   ☐ **1.** Fixing damaged eyesight using a laser.

   ☐ **2.** Printing body organs on an ink-jet printer.

   ☐ **3.** Creating new heart tissue from an individual's own cells.

   ☐ **4.** Replacing skin that has scars with skin from another place on the body.

   ☐ **5.** Replacing a damaged leg with a donated leg.

READING SKILL Skimming

Skimming is letting your eyes glide through a text as you read quickly. A reader **skims** a text when he or she wants to get a general idea about the information contained in a text but does not need to know full details.

For example, skimming is useful when a reader:

   a. wants to see if the full text is worth reading.

   b. wants to find key facts about a subject.

   c. wants to know the outcome or status of a current event.

   d. is writing a term paper and has to look through dozens of sources.

   e. wants to know which movies or restaurants the local newspaper recommends.

   f. has only a few minutes to review a business report before a meeting.

   g. is reading a story and cannot wait to find out what happens in the end.

To skim:

   1. Read the title and any subtitles.

   2. Read the first one or two paragraphs.

   3. Read the first and/or last sentence of the other paragraphs.

   4. Look quickly over the body of the other paragraphs, reading only a few words here and there. You may note names, places, dates and numbers, and words in bold or italic print.

   5. Read the last paragraph.

2 | Skimming

REMEMBER
Skimming a text will help you identify the topic and main idea. There is no need for a separate preview.

A. Skim the online article below in four minutes or less. Then answer the questions with a partner.

1. According to the text, what do scientists think they will be able to do one day?

_____

2. What do scientists use to do the technology mentioned in the text?

_____

3. What is one name for the new technology?

_____

4. Has the technology been perfected yet?

_____

5. What kind of impact can this technology have?

_____

B. Answer the questions with a partner.

1. What is the topic of this text?

2. What is the main idea of this text?

3 | Reading and Recalling

A. Read the text. Stop after each paragraph and tell a partner two things that you remember about it.

"Organ Printing" Could Drastically Change Medicine

1   What if the tens of thousands of people in the United States alone who are waiting for organ transplants didn't have to wait? What if accident victims could replace their scars with skin that was just like their own? What if someone who was missing an arm or a leg could replace it with one that felt, looked, and behaved exactly like the original?

2   Scientists say they have found a way to do all of these things and more with the use of a technology found in many American homes: an ink-jet printer. Researchers around the world say that by using this new technology, they can actually "print" living human tissue[1], and that one day they will be able to print entire organs.

continued

---
[1] **tissue:** similar cells that act together, such as muscles, skin, nerves, etc.

continued

3   Dr. Vladimir Mironov, of the Medical University of South Carolina, is a leading researcher in the field[2]. He says, "The promise of … 'organ printing' is very clear: we want to print living, three-dimensional[3] human organs."

4   **The Many Names for "Organ Printing"**
Though the field is young, it has already acquired a number of names: "bio-printing," "organ printing," "computer-aided tissue engineering," and "bio-manufacturing" are all terms that are used to describe the technology, according to Mironov. The most common term, however, is "organ printing." The technique is simple in concept but very complex and challenging to do.

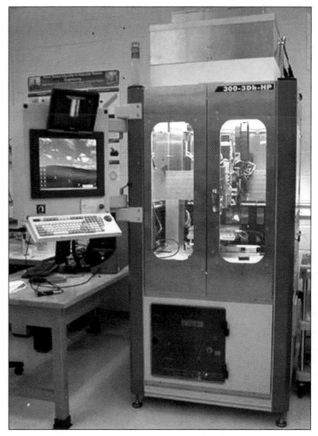

5   According to Thomas Boland, associate professor at Clemson University, researchers use an actual ink-jet printer, but they make some changes. The paper is replaced by a petri dish[4] that has a special liquid in it. The ink is replaced by a mixture of cells and a chemical called a "crosslinker." The crosslinker reacts with the liquid in the petri dish and causes it to gel[5], which creates a soft surface (and which replaces the paper). Thus, the printer is able to print the cells onto the gel surface. And the process can be repeated over and over, building layer upon layer, creating three dimensions.

6   **Limitations and Obstacles**
Right now, scientists can only create tissue about two inches (five centimeters) thick. Their immediate goal is to develop the technology that will allow them to print thicker tissue. According to Boland, thicker tissues require blood vessels. In all organs, it is the blood vessels that keep them alive and allow them to work properly. Without blood vessels, an organ will die. Therefore, when printing very thick tissues, it will be necessary to develop the technology to "print" the blood vessels, as well.

7   Boland is optimistic. He says, "In the future—maybe 50 years from now—we will be able to make very complex organs and bones, and very complex tissues."

continued

---

[2] **field:** a specialized area of professional or academic importance

[3] **three-dimensional:** having depth in its form; not flat

[4] **petri dish:** a shallow, round dish, used for growing bacteria in laboratories

[5] **to gel:** to change a liquid into a partially solid material (like jelly)

8   One of the current problems that occur with organ transplants is that a body often rejects the donated organ. However, when researchers have developed the technology that will allow them to print thicker tissues with blood vessels, doctors and patients will no longer need to worry about rejection. Since each tissue is printed according to an individual's own tissue, the replacement part will be just like a part from the individual's own body.

9   **An Important Impact**
     Although we may be a half-century away from being able to print entire organs, scientists say we are likely much closer to applications that will affect everyone's life. For example, Boland is working with colleagues to build tissue to repair a heart that has been damaged.

10   "The problem with heart tissue is that you can't generate your own heart cells anymore," explains Boland. People are born with a fixed number of heart cells. Therefore, if the heart is damaged, the body does not produce new cells to repair it.

11   Mironov said there are also researchers working with two-dimensional bio-printed materials for work with drugs and chemical tests. Imagine living patches of skin that could be used to test medicines or even cosmetics.

12   Indeed, as scientists and researchers work to perfect organ printing, Mironov understands well what this can mean for all of mankind. It can change medicine and the human life cycle forever.

B. Read the text again without pausing. Tell your partner two new things that you remember.

C. Work as a class or in large groups. Try to name as many things as you can about the text.

4 | Understanding the Text

A. Answer as many questions as you can without looking at the text. Discuss your answers with a partner.

1. What do researchers say they can do with an ink-jet printer? _____

_____

2. What is a current limitation of this process? _____

_____

3. What will be the main benefit? _____

_____

B. Check (✔) the procedures that may be possible one day because of organ printing according to the text.

☐ 1. replacing a missing arm or leg

☐ 2. printing entire organs

☐ 3. curing serious diseases

☐ 4. printing blood vessels

☐ 5. helping a person who has lost his or her hearing to hear again

5 | Understanding the Topic, Main Idea, and Supporting Details

A. Text. Answer the questions and discuss your answers with a partner.

1. What is the topic of the text? _____

2. What is the main idea of the text? _____

3. Are your answers for the topic and main idea here the same as the ones you chose after you previewed the text, or are your answers different? _____

B. Paragraphs. Answer the questions and write *MI* for *Main Idea* and *SD* for *Supporting Detail*. Discuss your answers with a partner.

1. What is the topic of ¶5? _____

2. What is the main idea and which are the supporting details for ¶5?

a. _____ The paper is replaced by a petri dish that has a special liquid in it.

b. _____ The ink is replaced by a mixture of cells and a chemical called a "crosslinker."

c. _____ The printer is able to print the cells onto the gel surface.

d. _____ To print human tissue, researchers use an ink-jet printer but make some changes.

e. _____ The process can be repeated over and over, building layer upon layer, creating three dimensions.

3. What is the topic of ¶6? _____

4. What is the main idea and which are the supporting details for ¶6?

a. _____ Scientists can only create tissue about two inches (five centimeters) thick.

b. _____ Blood vessels keep the organs alive and allow them to function properly.

c. _____ Without blood vessels, an organ will die.

d. _____ Scientists' goal is to develop the technology that will allow them to print thicker tissue with blood vessels.

5. What is the topic of ¶8? _____

6. What is the main idea and which are the supporting details for ¶8?

    a. _____ When researchers have developed the technology that will allow them to print thicker tissues with blood vessels, organ rejection will no longer be a problem.

    b. _____ A body often rejects, or refuses, a donated organ.

    c. _____ Since each tissue is printed according to an individual's own tissue, the replacement part will be just like a part from the individual's own body.

6 | Understanding Vocabulary in Context

A. Collocations. Complete the chart and then fill in the blanks. Discuss your answers with a partner.

1. Write the correct noun next to each adjective. Then match each collocation with its definition.

Adjective		Noun	Definition
_____ 1. common _____		researcher	a. number that doesn't change
_____ 2. leading _____		number	b. expression that is usual
_____ 3. fixed _____		term	c. well known scientist

2. Fill in the blanks with the correct collocation from the chart.

    a. Dr. Vladimir Mironov, of the Medical University of South Carolina, is a _____ in the field.

    b. Though the field is young, it has already acquired a number of names. ... The most _____, however, is "organ printing."

    c. "The problem with heart tissue is that you can't generate your own heart cells anymore," explains Boland. People are born with a _____ of heart cells.

B. Context Clues. Match each word or phrase on the left with the best definition on the right according to the text. Discuss your answers with a partner.

_____ 1. to acquire (¶4)   a. to refuse

_____ 2. to reject (¶8)   b. to produce; to make

_____ 3. to generate (¶10)   c. to fix

_____ 4. to repair (¶10)   d. to improve

_____ 5. to perfect (¶12)   e. to get; to collect

7 | Reading Critically—Fact and Opinion

Write *F* for *Fact* and *O* for *Opinion*. Discuss your answers with a partner.

___O___ 1. Organ printing is simple in concept but very complex and challenging to do. (¶4)

_____ 2. Right now, scientists can only create tissue about two inches (5 cm) thick. (¶6)

_____ 3. We may be a half-century away from being able to print entire organs. (¶9)

_____ 4. If the heart is damaged, the body does not produce new cells to repair it. (¶10)

_____ 5. Organ printing can change medicine and the human life cycle forever. (¶12)

8 | Discussing the Issues

Answer the questions and discuss your answers with a partner.

1. In what ways could organ printing change the human life cycle?

2. In your opinion, what is the most interesting possibility with organ printing?

3. Would you accept an ink-jet transplant? Why or why not?

Text 3 | History of Cloning

1 | Getting Started

Check (✔) whether you agree or disagree with each statement.

Statement	Agree	Disagree
1. All scientific research is important and necessary.	☐	☐
2. Scientists are careful about the research that they do.	☐	☐
3. Cloning animals is an important kind of scientific research.	☐	☐
4. Scientists should research ways to clone humans.	☐	☐
5. Governments should control scientific research.	☐	☐

GRAPHICS Understanding Timelines

Timelines show a sequence of chronological events over a specific period of time. Timelines can be drawn vertically—like the one on the next page—or horizontally. **Preview** timelines by reading the title, any subtitles, the first date and event, and the last date and event.

2 | Active Previewing

Preview the timeline below and then answer the questions. Discuss your answers with a partner.

1. What is the topic of this timeline?

2. Approximately how many years does this timeline cover?

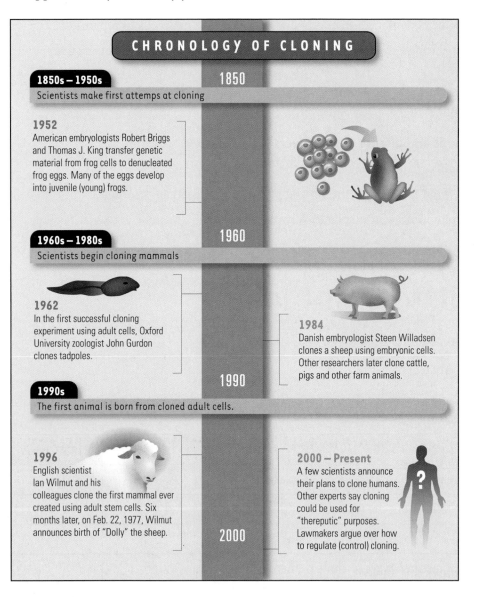

CHRONOLOGY OF CLONING

1850

1850s – 1950s
Scientists make first attemps at cloning

1952
American embryologists Robert Briggs and Thomas J. King transfer genetic material from frog cells to denucleated frog eggs. Many of the eggs develop into juvenile (young) frogs.

1960

1960s – 1980s
Scientists begin cloning mammals

1962
In the first successful cloning experiment using adult cells, Oxford University zoologist John Gurdon clones tadpoles.

1984
Danish embryologist Steen Willadsen clones a sheep using embryonic cells. Other researchers later clone cattle, pigs and other farm animals.

1990

1990s
The first animal is born from cloned adult cells.

1996
English scientist Ian Wilmut and his colleagues clone the first mammal ever created using adult stem cells. Six months later, on Feb. 22, 1977, Wilmut announces birth of "Dolly" the sheep.

2000 – Present
A few scientists announce their plans to clone humans. Other experts say cloning could be used for "thereputic" purposes. Lawmakers argue over how to regulate (control) cloning.

2000

3 | Understanding the Graphics

Write each event from the vertical timeline on the horizontal timeline below.

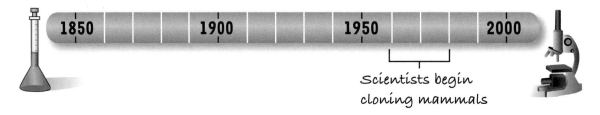

1850   1900   1950   2000

Scientists begin
cloning mammals

4 | Scanning

Scan the vertical timeline on the previous page for the answers to the questions. Discuss your answers with a partner.

1. When did scientists begin cloning mammals? <u>1960s-1980s</u>

2. What happened in 1962? _____

3. What did English scientist Ian Wilmut clone? _____

4. When did a few scientists announce their plans to clone humans? _____

5. What was cloned first: a tadpole or a sheep? _____

5 | Discussing the Issues

Answer the questions and discuss your answers with a partner.

1. Why do you think scientists cloned amphibians such as tadpoles and frogs before they cloned mammals?

2. Do you think cloning should be regulated? Why or why not?

3. What would be some of the advantages or disadvantages to cloning humans?

Text 4 | Ancient Surgery

1 | Getting Started

A. Answer the questions and briefly discuss your answers with a partner.

1. Have you ever seen an illustration similar to the one on the right?

2. What ancient civilization is related to this illustration?

3. Check (✔) the things this ancient civilization is famous for.

    ☐ a. building pyramids

    ☐ b. discovering America

    ☐ c. performing surgery

    ☐ d. wrapping mummies

    ☐ e. growing tea

B. Check (✔) the correct answers.

This procedure would be performed by a ...	... physician.	... surgeon.
1. cutting away damaged body tissue	☐	☐
2. sewing closed a small wound	☐	☐
3. repairing a broken arm	☐	☐
4. operating on a brain injury	☐	☐
5. changing the shape of someone's nose	☐	☐

2 | Skimming

A. Skim the magazine article on the next page in four minutes or less. Then answer the questions with a partner.

1. What did archaeologists find?

2. What was on the walls?

3. Who was Skar?

4. Who was Edwin Smith?

5. What is the papyrus a summary of?

B. Answer the questions with a partner.

1. What is the topic of this text?

2. What is the main idea of this text?

3 | Reading and Recalling

A. Read the text. Stop after each paragraph and tell a partner two things that you remember about it.

Signs of Surgery in Ancient Egypt

1   In November of 2001, in the shadow of the first royal pyramid at Saqqara (built around 2630 B.C.E. not far from Cairo), archaeologists made an amazing discovery. Under more than 16 feet (5 meters) of sand was a tomb[1] that had been hidden since 2000 B.C.E. The hieroglyphs—ancient Egyptian writing—on the walls of the tomb indicated that surgery was practiced in ancient Egypt. This is the first possible hard proof that surgery was actually performed so early.

2   The tomb belonged to Skar, the chief physician of one of Egypt's rulers of the 5th dynasty. It contained about 30 bronze medical implements, the oldest ever found, including scalpels[2], needles, and a spoon.

continued

---

[1] **tomb:** grave; place where someone is buried

[2] **scalpel:** knife used for surgery

First Proof of Surgical Knowledge

3 Egyptologists—historians who study ancient Egyptian culture—have known for a long time that Egyptians possessed the knowledge of surgery. The first suggestion that surgery may have been practiced in ancient times was discovered in the Egyptian city of Luxor in 1862.

4 In the 19th century, the American trader Edwin Smith spent much of his time in the Luxor markets. He was always looking for ancient artifacts[3] that he could sell for an easy profit. Smith even described himself as "an American farmer of Luxor." Many Egyptologists consider him to have been a dishonorable character.

5 Often, Smith was quite happy to buy a well made fake, and he did not worry about reselling it as the real thing. However, he knew his business, and he treated one ancient Egyptian document, a papyrus that looked genuine (real), very differently. Since he was able to read hieroglyphs, he could see that this was a description of medical practices and therefore highly unusual.

6 Although he could have gotten a good price for the papyrus, for unknown reasons Smith decided to keep it, and it remained in his family for more than 70 years. It was only when it was fully translated in the 1930s that its full significance was recognized. Today, it is known as the Edwin Smith Surgical Papyrus.

7 This papyrus is a detailed—although incomplete—summary of surgical treatments for wounds, starting with head injuries and working down the body. There are 48 case studies recorded in the papyrus, and a modern surgeon would be familiar with the way each case is described.

8 The papyrus goes into great detail describing each individual trauma[4]: how one would look at it, diagnose it, examine it, and finally treat it. It describes how to sew together a wound. For liquid-filled tumors, it recommends cauterization, the use of heat to destroy damaged tissue and close up blood vessels. Today, a similar technique is used, with an electric current taking the place of heat.

9 Even more important are the neurological insights that the Edwin Smith papyrus gives: it contains the first descriptions of the meninges (the membranes that cover the brain), the external surface of the brain, and the brain-spine fluid. It also notes that brain injuries are connected with changes in the function of other parts of the body, especially in the legs.

10 The papyrus was copied in about 1700 B.C.E. from an ancient composite[5] manuscript. In addition to the original author's text, written between 3000 and 2500 B.C.E., the papyrus contained 69 explanatory notes added a few hundred years later. The scribe who copied it made many errors, some of which he corrected in the margins. He had copied at least 18 columns of it, when, at the bottom of a column, he paused in the middle of a word and left the papyrus unfinished for all time.

Other Clues Relating to Ancient Egyptian Surgery

11 Other clues that tell us that the Egyptians had discovered the principles of surgery can be found in the way they prepared their dead. For instance, the mummy of the great pharaoh Ramses II, now in Cairo Museum, was surgically altered by having a small bone and a quantity of seeds inserted into his nose. In life, this had been his most prominent feature. The Egyptian surgeons ensured that, in death, it remained just as prominent.

12 The mummy of Queen Nunjmet was also enhanced. Her cheeks and belly were stuffed with bandages, resin, and a cheesy substance. Today, plastic surgeons would use materials such as silicon to fill out various body parts.

13 So the Egyptians used surgery on the dead. And, as the Edwin Smith papyrus shows, they had the skills to perform such operations on the living. But did they? The mummies don't reveal any evidence that proves this one way or the other.

---

[3] **artifact:** ancient object

[4] **trauma:** here, serious injury or wound

[5] **composite:** having several parts

B. Read the text again without pausing. Tell your partner two new pieces of information that you remember.

C. Work as a class or in large groups. Try to name as many things as you can about the text.

4 | Understanding the Text

A. Answer as many questions as you can without looking at the text. Discuss your answers with a partner.

1. Where is the papyrus from? _____

2. What does the papyrus describe? _____

3. Whom do we know the Egyptians practiced surgery on? _____

B. Write *T* for *True* and *F* for *False* according to the text.

_____ 1. Skar was a ruler of the 5th dynasty.

_____ 2. Edwin Smith was always looking for ancient artifacts that he could sell for an easy profit.

_____ 3. Edwin Smith sold the papyrus as soon as he found it.

_____ 4. The papyrus is a detailed summary of surgical treatments for wounds.

_____ 5. The principles of surgery cannot be found in the way the Egyptians prepared their dead.

5 | Understanding the Topic, Main Idea, and Supporting Details

A. Text. Answer the questions and discuss your answers with a partner.

1. What is the topic of the text?_____

2. What is the main idea of the text?_____

3. Are your answers for the topic and main idea here the same as the ones you determined after you previewed the text, or are your answers different? _____

B. Paragraphs. Write *MI* for *Main Idea* and *SD* for *Supporting Detail*. Discuss your answers with a partner.

1. What is the topic of ¶4? _____

2. What is the main idea and which are the supporting details of ¶4?

a. _____ Edwin Smith described himself as "an American farmer of Luxor."

b. _____ Edwin Smith spent a lot of time in the Luxor markets looking for artifacts he could sell for an easy profit.

c. _____ Many Egyptologists consider Edwin Smith to have been a dishonorable character.

3. What is the topic of ¶8? _____

4. What is the main idea and which are the supporting details of ¶8?

   a. _____ The papyrus describes how to stitch together a wound.

   b. _____ The papyrus describes how to use heat to destroy damaged tissue and close up blood vessels.

   c. _____ The papyrus describes medical injuries and their treatments.

5. What is the topic of ¶11?_____

6. What is the main idea and which are the supporting details of ¶11?

   a. _____ The mummy of the great pharaoh Ramses II was surgically altered.

   b. _____ Other clues that tell us that the Egyptians had discovered the principles of surgery can be found in the way they prepared their dead.

   c. _____ The Egyptian surgeons ensured that, in death, pharoah Ramses II's nose remained just as prominent as it had been in life.

6 | Understanding Vocabulary in Context

A. Collocations. Complete the chart and then fill in the blanks. Discuss your answers with a partner.

1. Write the correct noun next to each adjective. Then match each collocation with its definition.

Adjective		Noun	Definition
_____ 1. hard _____		thing	a. complete explanation
_____ 2. easy _____		detail	b. true or authentic object
_____ 3. real _____		significance	c. money gotten with little effort
_____ 4. full _____		proof	d. evidence that something is true
_____ 5. great _____		profit	e. extreme importance

2. Fill in the blanks with the correct collocation from the chart.

   a. The hieroglyphs ... on the walls of the tomb indicated that surgery was practiced in ancient Egypt. This is the first possible _____ that surgery was actually performed so early.

   b. ... the American trader Edwin Smith spent much of his time in the Luxor markets. He was always looking for ancient artifacts that he could sell for an _____.

   c. Often, Smith was quite happy to buy a well made fake, and he did not worry about reselling it as the _____.

d. Although he could have gotten a good price for the papyrus, for unknown reasons Smith decided to keep it, and it remained in his family for more than 70 years. It was only when it was fully translated in the 1930s that its _____ was recognized.

e. The papyrus goes into _____ describing each individual trauma: how one would look at it, diagnose it, examine it, and finally treat it.

B. Context Clues. Select the best meaning for each word or phrase according to the text. Discuss your answers with a partner.

1. to possess (¶**3**)

a. to look for   b. to build   c. to have

2. manuscript (¶**10**)

a. a document; something written

b. a speech; something spoken

c. a sketch; something drawn

3. to be stuffed (¶**12**)

a. to be cut   b. to be filled   c. to be covered

7 | Reading Critically—Fact and Opinion

Write *F* for *Fact* and *O* for *Opinion*. Discuss your answers with a partner.

___F___ **1.** The first royal pyramid at Saqqara was built around 2630 B.C.E. (¶**1**)

_____ **2.** The writing on the wall of the tomb is the first possible hard proof that surgery was actually performed by the ancient Egyptians. (¶**1**)

_____ **3.** Many Egyptologists consider Edwin Smith to have been a dishonorable character. (¶**4**)

_____ **4.** There are 48 case studies recorded in the papyrus. (¶**7**)

_____ **5.** The papyrus also notes that brain injuries are connected with changes in the function of other parts of the body. (¶**9**)

8 | Discussing the Issues

Answer the questions and discuss your answers with a partner.

1. Do you find it surprising that such an ancient people had knowledge of surgery? Why or why not?

2. Do you think doctors today could learn something about medicine by reading ancient medical documents? Why or why not?

3. Why do you think that so many people are fascinated by ancient Egypt?

Putting It On Paper

A. Write a paragraph on one of these topics.

1. Would it be a good thing if scientists succeeded in cloning an extinct animal?

2. How can technological advances in medicine improve or worsen quality of life?

Steps for your paragraph

a. In your first sentence, clearly state your opinion about the topic.

b. In your supporting sentences, use specific examples that will support your opinion.

c. Be sure to include at least one cause and one effect in your paragraph.

B. Exchange paragraphs with a partner. First, read your partner's paragraph and answer the questions in the checklist. Then give feedback to your partner.

✔ CHECKLIST
1. Does the first sentence clearly show which topic your partner chose?
2. Do the following sentences give specific examples that support or illustrate the topic?
3. Does the paragraph show clearly your partner's point of view about his or her topic?
4. Does the paragraph contain at least one cause and one effect?
5. Is there any information in the paragraph that is not related to your partner's topic? If yes, please underline it on your partner's paper, and write it below:

_____

_____

_____

_____

_____

_____

_____

C. Revise your paragraph based on your partner's feedback.

Taking It Online | Scientific Firsts

A. With a partner, use the Internet to research two "scientific firsts."

1. Use Google (www.google.com) or another major search engine to find Websites with information about two of the following "firsts":

anesthesia discovered   dinosaur bones found

animal cloned   heart transplant performed

artificial heart created   penicillin discovered

2. Preview the Websites.

ONLINE TIP

Search with a simple word form or word part for more inclusive results: "clone" (not "cloned").

B. Complete the tables with the information you find.

Scientific first:	successful kidney transplant performed
Website address(es):	http://www.pbs.org/wgbh/aso/databank/entries/dm54ki.html
Who participated in this "first"? Richard Herrick received the transplant. His twin brother Ronald donated a kidney. Dr. Joseph Murray performed the operation.	
When did it happen? 1954	
Where did it happen? Peter Bent Brigham Hospital in Boston	

Scientific first:	
Website address(es):	
Who participated in this "first"?	
When did it happen?	
Where did it happen?	

Scientific first:	
Website address(es):	
Who participated in this "first"?	
When did it happen?	
Where did it happen?	

C. Following up. Choose one of your "scientific firsts." Create a timeline that shows the events leading up to and/or following the "first." Do additional Internet research if necessary.

Chapter 8

The Science of Addiction

READING SKILL
- Reviewing Reading Skills

VOCABULARY STRATEGY
- Reviewing Vocabulary Strategies

GRAPHICS
- Reviewing Tables

Answer the questions and briefly discuss your answers with a partner.

1. Is it possible to be addicted to hobbies?

2. What are some activities that people can be addicted to?

3. Look at the photos. What does each photo show?

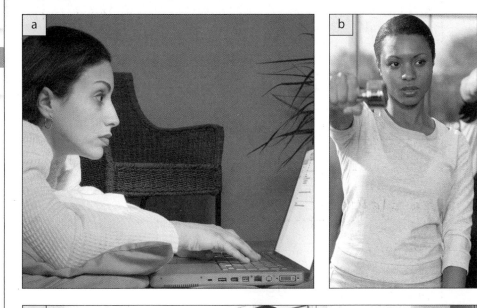

Text 1 | Addicted to the Internet

1 | Getting Started

A. Answer the questions and briefly discuss your answers with a partner.

1. Do you use the Internet?

2. What are some reasons that people use the Internet?

3. What personal problems, if any, can result from excessive Internet use?

B. Check (✔) whether you agree or disagree with each statement. Briefly discuss your answers with a partner.

Statement	Agree	Disagree
1. People can become addicted to the Internet.	☐	☐
2. Excessive Internet users experience more anxiety than moderate Internet users do.	☐	☐
3. Excessive Internet users have different personality traits from moderate Internet users.	☐	☐
4. People use the Internet as a way to escape from their everyday problems.	☐	☐
5. Excessive Internet users might experience mental problems.	☐	☐

2 | Active Previewing

A. Preview the newspaper article on the next page by reading the first three paragraphs. Then answer the questions with a partner.

1. What can harm your mental health?

2. Where was the research published?

3. What is this phenomenon called?

B. Answer these questions with a partner.

1. What is the topic of this text?

2. What is the main idea of this text?

3 | Reading and Recalling

A. Read the text. Stop after each paragraph and tell a partner two things that you remember about it.

Addicted to the Internet

BY IAN MACLEOD

1. Too much Internet use can harm your mental health, a new medical study suggests.

2. Research published in the Canadian Journal of Psychiatry[1] supports a growing body of evidence that the interactive and dynamic nature of the Internet—from virtual gaming and chat rooms to news groups and music downloading—is associated with serious handicaps (problems) to the personalities of people who overuse it.

3. There is no official classification, or name, for an extreme preoccupation with the Internet. However, many medical professionals have dubbed[2] the phenomenon "Internet addiction." They consider it to be a psychological dependence similar to a gambling addiction.

4. The latest study, by researchers at Korea's Dong-A University College of Medicine and the Harvard Medical School, now links the addiction to adverse psychiatric symptoms such as hostility (extreme unfriendliness) and obsessive-compulsiveness[3].

5. But big unanswered questions remain: Are the adverse psychiatric conditions a *result* of excessive Internet use or do they *precede* it? And can a person's personality make him more likely to be addicted to the Internet?

6. The Korean-U.S. research team ranked, or ordered, 328 Korean senior high school students in terms of their weekly Internet use in the previous month. Sixteen students were classified as excessive users, logging on an average of about 19 hours a week. Fifty-nine students reported no Internet use. Male students significantly outnumbered female students in both the moderate and excessive user groups.

7. In addition to hostility and obsessive-compulsiveness, the excessive Internet users were found to experience more serious psychological problems, including paranoia, depression, anger, impulsiveness[4], worry, and phobias (fears). The study also found the students who made excessive use of the Internet appeared to have personality traits distinctive from the students with modest and minimal Internet use.

8. The study was far from perfect—it had limitations, including a small sample size and use of questionnaires rather than direct, in-depth interviews. However, the study concluded that people with inner conflicts might use the Internet as a way to relax, and students with these conflicts may use the Internet to balance the psychological pain in their personalities. This finding supports at least one previous study that found that the Internet is used by some people already experiencing poor social relationships, dissatisfaction with their physical appearance and poor coping skills.

9. In 2003, University of Florida psychiatrists published guidelines to help doctors determine when Web use is too extreme to be healthy. Dr. Nathan Shapira, an assistant professor of psychiatry, wrote diagnostic criteria[5] after conducting psychiatric evaluations of 20 volunteers who identified themselves as having problems with the Internet, and 17 randomly selected college students with varying levels of Internet use.

10. The University of Florida reported that volunteers who called themselves problematic Internet users tended to have pre-existing psychiatric problems such as bipolar disorder, depression or alcohol abuse.

11. These test subjects were online more than 30 hours per week, and their non essential Internet use was ten times greater than their essential Internet use, such as job- and school-related activities—28 hours compared with 2.8 hours.

12. Regardless of their reasons for using the Internet, heavy users should be aware of the problems that may be connected with such excessive use.

---

[1] **psychiatry:** the study and treatment of mental disorders

[2] **to dub:** to name

[3] **obsessive-compulsiveness:** a personality trait where a person relieves anxiety by repeating specific acts or tasks

[4] **impulsiveness:** acting on a desire without considering the result(s)

[5] **diagnostic criteria:** the process used to determine the signs or symptoms of a disease or illness

B. Read the text again without pausing. Tell your partner two new things that you remember.

C. Work as a class or in large groups. Try to name as many things as you can about the text.

4 | Understanding the Text

A. Answer as many questions as you can without looking at the text. Discuss your answers with a partner.

1. What addiction is discussed in this text? _addiction to the internet_

2. What problems is this addiction linked to? _heavy internet users_

3. In which ways do the people with this addiction differ from people who don't have the addiction? _they use it in longer hours_

B. Complete the chart according to the text. Discuss your answers with a partner.

Personality traits or conditions related to excessive Internet use
1. _Psychological problems_
2. _paranoia_
3. _anger_
4. _worry_
5. _depression_

5 | Understanding the Topic and Main Idea

Answer the questions. Discuss your answers with a partner.

1. What is the topic of the text? _Addicted to the internet_

2. What is the main idea of the text? _~~showing the~~ some people get addicted to the internet_

3. Are your answers for the topic and main idea here the same as the ones you determined after you previewed the text, or are your answers different? _yes_

6 | Understanding Pronouns and Possessive Adjectives

Write what each pronoun and possessive adjective refers to according to the text.

1. your (your mental health) (¶1) _the reader_

2. it (people who overuse it) (¶2) _____

3. they (do they precede it) (¶5) _____

4. him (make him more likely to be addicted) (¶5) _____

5. their (their weekly Internet use) (¶6) _____

6. it (it had limitations) (¶8) _____

7. their (their personalities) (¶8) _____

8. their (their non essential Internet use) (¶11) _____

7 | Understanding Vocabulary in Context

A. Synonyms. Write the best synonym for each word or phrase according to the text.

1. handicap (¶2) _problem_____

2. classification (¶3) _____

3. hostility (¶4) _____

4. to rank (¶6) _____

5. phobia (¶7) _____

B. Examples. Write examples from the text for each word or phrase. Discuss your answers with a partner.

1. adverse psychiatric symptoms (¶4) _hostility and obsessive-compulsiveness_____

2. limitations (¶8) _____

3. essential Internet use (¶11) _____

8 | Reading Critically—Fact and Opinion

Write *F* for *Fact* and *O* for *Opinion*. Discuss your answers with a partner.

___F___ 1. Fifty-nine students reported no Internet use. (¶6)

_____ 2. The study was far from perfect. (¶8)

_____ 3. These test subjects were online more than 30 hours per week. (¶11)

9 | Discussing the Issues

Answer the questions and discuss your answers with a partner.

1. Do psychiatric conditions lead to excessive Internet use or does Internet use lead to psychiatric conditions? Explain.

2. What other physical or mental problems can Internet addiction cause?

3. Imagine you have a friend who is addicted to the Internet. What are some suggestions you can give your friend for reducing the number of hours he or she spends online?

Text 2 | Work-Out Addiction

1 | Getting Started

A. Answer the questions and briefly discuss your answers with a partner.

1. Do you ever work out at the gym or lift weights?

2. How much exercise is too much exercise?

3. What do you think could happen if a person exercises too much?

B. Check (✔) the reasons that people exercise.

Reasons for exercising	Physical	Psychological	Both
1. because it makes them feel good	☐	☐	☐
2. in order to cope with stress	☐	☐	☐
3. in order to lose weight	☐	☐	☐
4. because it makes them healthier	☐	☐	☐
5. because they are dependent on it or addicted to it	☐	☐	☐

2 | Active Previewing

Preview the magazine article on the next page. Underline the title, the first sentence of each paragraph, and the last sentence of the text as you preview. Then answer the questions with a partner.

1. What is the topic of this text?

2. What is the main idea of this text?

3 | Reading and Recalling

A. Read the text. Stop after each paragraph and tell a partner two things that you remember about it.

Exercise Addiction Affects Campuses

1 Loud music blares overhead and drowns out the noise of the machines. A girl fixes her messy blonde hair. It is 11 a.m. at the West Virginia University Student Recreation Center, and the upstairs workout room is slowly filling up.

2 Looking around, the girl straightens her white T-shirt before picking up two large hand weights. She positions herself in front of the mirror on the wall and watches herself as she slowly maneuvers the weights above her head, one at a time. A drop of sweat begins to roll slowly down her face.

3 Siera McDonald, another student at the university who calls herself an exercise addict, is familiar with this scene. "As human creatures, our bodies are meant to be moved and used. In my perfect life[1], I would be outside using my body for two to three hours a day," she said.

4 No one doubts the benefits of daily exercise and a healthy lifestyle. However, sometimes people take exercise to the extreme[2], developing a dependence on or compulsion[3] for exercise. A disruption describes a situation that interrupts something or creates confusion. And exercise can become such a problem that it becomes a disruption in a person's daily activities.

5 Although doctors and experts debate the seriousness of this physical and psychological affliction, they all agree that for some people, exercise can become more than just a way to stay healthy and fit.

6 More than anything, health professionals debate what to call this problem. "Exercise dependence" and "exercise addiction" are the most common terms used to describe this behavior, but some feel these titles do not correctly describe the problem. "There are a lot of people who say it isn't a dependence or it's not a real addiction, so it should be called compulsive exercise or obligatory[4] exercise," said Dr. Jan Melcher, a Carruth Center counselor who has worked with patients with exercise problems.

7 Whatever one chooses to call it, all these terms describe a fairly new phenomenon in which people become dependent on exercise. Obsessive exercisers feel exercise is necessary to cope with the stresses of daily life. In serious cases, people experience withdrawal symptoms[5] as a result of decreasing or skipping their exercise entirely. Often, they exercise despite illnesses and injuries, and other areas of their lives suffer because of the dependence. For many people, exercise begins to take up an increasingly larger chunk of time as they spend more and more time at the gym. "It's a constant battle with time. Fitting it into the day is a challenge," said McDonald, who admits, however, that she would never pass on dinner with friends to exercise.

continued

---

[1] **in a/one's perfect life:** in a perfect situation

[2] **to take something to the extreme:** to do too much of something

[3] **compulsion:** a strong desire to do something, even against one's will

[4] **obligatory:** necessary; required

[5] **withdrawal symptom:** physical and psychological reaction that occurs in someone who is deprived of an addictive substance

continued

8   There are two theories to explain why people might develop an addiction to exercise: the social theory and the endorphin theory.

9   The social theory suggests that exercise addiction sometimes starts when an individual includes exercise in his or her life in order to improve some aspect of it, such as weight, stress, or fitness. Then the exercise routine gets taken to the extreme. Not exercising begins to make the person feel guilty, so he or she then needs to start working out every day in order to avoid the guilty feelings.

10   The endorphin theory discusses the problem from a physical point of view. Endorphins are chemicals released by the body after physical activity, and they make a person feel good. The endorphin theory argues that people become dependent on exercise because it is a way to maintain this positive mood. In order to preserve the mood, they must continue exercising, much like the effect of a drug.

11   A recent study conducted at the University of Wisconsin–Madison gives even more credibility to the endorphin theory. A craving refers to a strong desire or need for something. It is what drug addicts experience when they do not have drugs. Interestingly, the study showed that, like drug addicts, mice that have been deprived of their running wheels crave exercise. This craving activates their brains in the same way that any other craving does. Whether this finding applies to humans must still be studied, but it does lend support to the theory that exercise can be addictive.

B. Read the text again without pausing. Tell your partner two new things that you remember.

C. Work as a class or in large groups. Try to name as many things as you can about the text.

4 | Understanding the Text

A. Answer as many questions as you can without looking at the text. Discuss your answers with a partner.

1. What are the people described in the text addicted to? _____

2. How does the problem affect the lives of the people in the text? _____

_____

3. What can happen if addicts stop doing this activity? _____

_____

B. Complete the sentences according to the text.

1. Sometimes people take exercise to the extreme, developing a(n) _____ it.

   a. affection for   b. dislike for   c. dependence on

2. _____ debate what to call the problem of exercise dependence.

   a. Health professionals   b. Sports people   c. Scientists

3. The _____ theory suggests that people exercise more and more in order to avoid the guilt they feel if they don't exercise.

    a. exercise   b. social   c. endorphin

4. The _____ theory argues that people become dependent on exercise because it is a way to maintain the positive mood these chemicals create.

    a. addiction   b. endorphin   c. social

5. A study at the University of Wisconsin–Madison showed that _____ that have been deprived of their physical activity crave exercise.

    a. rabbits   b. dogs   c. mice

5 | Understanding the Topic, Main Idea, and Supporting Details

A. Text. Answer the questions and discuss your answers with a partner.

1. What is the topic of the text? _____

2. What is the main idea of the text? _____

3. Are your answers for the topic and main idea here the same as the ones you determined after you previewed the text, or are your answers different? _____

B. Paragraphs. Answer the following questions and write *MI* for *Main Idea* and *SD* for *Supporting Detail*. Discuss your answers with a partner.

1. What is the topic of ¶6? _____

2. What is the main idea and which are the supporting details for ¶6?

    a. _____ "Exercise dependency" and "exercise addiction" are the most common terms.

    b. _____ Many people say exercise dependency isn't a dependence or a real addiction.

    c. _____ Health professionals debate what to call this exercise problem.

3. What is the topic of ¶7? _____

4. What is the main idea and which are the supporting details for ¶7?

    a. _____ Obsessive exercisers feel exercise is necessary to cope with the stresses of daily life.

    b. _____ In serious cases, people experience withdrawal symptoms when exercise is decreased or skipped entirely.

    c. _____ Often, [exercise addicts] exercise despite illnesses and injuries, and other areas of their lives suffer because of the dependence.

    d. _____ Exercise dependency is a fairly new phenomenon.

    e. _____ For many people, exercise begins to take up an increasingly larger chunk of time as they spend more and more time at the gym.

5. What is the topic of ¶10? _____

6. What is the main idea of ¶10? _____

7. What are two supporting details for ¶10? _____

_____

_____

6 | Understanding Vocabulary in Context

A. Definitions. Write the definition for each word or phrase according to the text. Discuss your answers with a partner

1. disruption (¶4) _a situation that interrupts something or creates confusion_

2. endorphin (¶10) _____

3. craving (¶11) _____

B. Context Clues. Select the best meaning for each word or phrase according to the text. Discuss your answers with a partner.

1. to blare (¶1)

   a. to fix   b. to play loudly   c. to fill

2. to maneuver something (¶2)

   a. to move something carefully   b. to look at   c. to drop heavily

3. affliction (¶5)

   a. professional, expert   b. exercise program   c. trouble, misfortune

7 | Reading Critically

A. Cause and Effect. Read the sentences. Label the cause *C* and the effect *E*. Discuss your answers with a partner.

1. In serious cases, people experience withdrawal symptoms as a result of decreasing or skipping their exercise entirely. (¶7)

   __E__ a. In serious cases, people experience withdrawal symptoms.

   __C__ b. People decrease or skip their exercise entirely.

2. Not exercising begins to make the person feel guilty, so he or she then needs to start working out every day ... (¶9)

   _____ a. Not exercising begins to make the person feel guilty.

   _____ b. The person then needs to start working out every day.

3. The endorphin theory argues that people become dependent on exercise because it is a way to maintain this positive mood. (¶10)

   _____ a. The endorphin theory argues that people become dependent on exercise.

   _____ b. Exercise is a way to maintain this positive mood.

B. Fact and Opinion. Write *F* for *Fact* and *O* for *Opinion*. Discuss your answers with a partner.

___O___ 1. No one doubts the benefits of daily exercise and a healthy lifestyle. (¶4)

_____ 2. For some people, exercise can become more than just a way to stay healthy and fit. (¶5)

_____ 3. Dr. Jan Melcher is a Carruth Center counselor who has worked with patients with exercise problems. (¶6)

_____ 4. Exercise is necessary to cope with the stresses of daily life. (¶7)

_____ 5. Endorphins are chemicals released by the body after physical activity. (¶10)

8 | Discussing the Issues

Answer the questions and discuss your answers with a partner.

1. How much exercise do you think people should get, if any?

2. Do you think it's reasonable to refer to a dependence on exercise as an addiction? Why or why not?

3. If you thought a friend were addicted to exercise, what would you do?

Text 3 | Television Addiction

1 | Getting Started

Answer the questions and briefly discuss your answers with a partner.

1. How often do you watch television?

   a. never   b. 1-2 hours a week   c. 1 hour a day   d. 4+ hours a day

2. Check (✔) the statements that describe your television-watching habits.

   ☐ a. The TV set remains off.

   ☐ b. The TV is off unless I am watching a program.

   ☐ c. I watch programs, but I also "channel surf" during commercial breaks.

   ☐ d. The TV is usually on, but I change channels frequently.

3. What are your social habits? Circle the number that expresses how much you agree or disagree with each statement.

a. I have many hobbies and interests.

Strongly Disagree		Neutral		Strongly Agree
1	2	3	4	5

b. Watching TV is my favorite hobby.

Strongly Disagree		Neutral		Strongly Agree
1	2	3	4	5

c. I have good eating and exercise habits.

Strongly Disagree		Neutral		Strongly Agree
1	2	3	4	5

d. I read a lot for pleasure.

Strongly Disagree		Neutral		Strongly Agree
1	2	3	4	5

2 | Active Previewing

Preview the table on the next page and then answer the questions. Briefly discuss your answers with a partner.

1. What is the title of this table? _____

2. What are the three row headings? _____

_____

_____

3. What is the topic of this table? _____

_____

_____

_____

> **REMEMBER**
> Preview a table by reading the title, the column and/or row headings, and any **boldfaced** information. For more on *previewing tables*, see page 78.

The Kaufman Spectrum of Television Addiction

	Phase 0	Phase 1	Phase 2	Phase 3
Viewing Frequency	No TV watching	Sporadic TV watching (watch one or two particular shows each week)	Moderate TV watching (watch at least one program per day)	Heavy TV watching (more than four hours per day)
Television Habits	TV set remains off	Programs are watched in their entirety, then TV set is turned off	Will research programs before watching Balance between watching entire programs and channel surfing	Watch TV out of habit, not interest Heavy channel changing
Social Habits	Involved with many non-TV activities Have many hobbies and interests Read a lot	Watch TV out of interest and curiosity Many non-TV interests and hobbies Enjoy reading	Watching TV high on list of favorite activities Will plan social activities around TV schedule	Frequent feelings of boredom Will opt out of social events to watch television Poor diet, exercise, and reading habits

3 | Scanning

Scan the table for the answers to the questions. Discuss your answers with a partner.

1. In which phase do people watch TV out of interest and curiosity? __Phase 1__

2. How many hours of TV do people in Phase 3 watch? _____

3. What are the television habits of people in Phase 0? _____

4. In which phase do people plan social activities around the TV schedule? _____

5. What is the viewing frequency for people in Phase 1? _____

4 | Discussing the Issues

Answer the questions and discuss your answers with a partner.

1. What are some advantages and disadvantages of watching television?

2. In what ways can watching a lot of television affect a person's life?

3. What are some ways that a television addict could decrease the amount of time he or she spends watching television?

Text 4 | Cell Phone Addiction

1 | Getting Started

A. Answer the questions, and briefly discuss your answers with a partner.

1. Do you own a cell phone?

2. For what purposes do you, or people you know, use a cell phone?

3. Can cell phone use be an addiction for some people? Why or why not?

B. Check (✔) whether the following uses for the cell phone are reasonable or not reasonable.

This cell phone use is ...	... reasonable.	... unreasonable.
1. calling someone to say you will be late	☐	☐
2. answering your phone while you are at the movies	☐	☐
3. leaving your cell phone on during dinner	☐	☐
4. sending a text message to a friend while you are waiting in line at the market	☐	☐
5. answering your cell phone in class or during a business meeting	☐	☐

2 | Skimming

A. Skim the academic text on the next page in five minutes or less. Then answer the questions with a partner.

> **REMEMBER**
> Skimming a text will help you identify the topic and main idea of a text. There is no need for a separate preview.

1. What could be becoming a problem?

   _____

2. Who do cell phones interfere with?

   _____

3. How are problems with cell phone use different from addictions to alcohol, drugs, or gambling?

   _____

4. Who cannot get by without cell phones?

_____

_____

5. What is one solution to overcome cell phone abuse?

_____

_____

B. Answer the questions with a partner.

1. What is the topic of this text?

2. What is the main idea of this text?

3 | Reading and Recalling

A. Read the text. Stop after each paragraph and tell a partner two things that you remember about it.

Is Cell Phone Use Becoming a Major Problem?

1 "Turn off your cell phones and pagers." For most people, this warning is easy to follow: simply press a button. But for a growing number of people across the globe, the idea of being out of touch, even just for a 90-minute movie, is enough to cause stress, says a University of Florida (UF) psychologist who studies addictions to the Internet and other technologies.

2 **Cell Phone Interference**

Cellular phones were created to make modern life more convenient, but they're actually beginning to interfere[1] in the lives of some users because they don't know when to turn them off, says Lisa Merlo, an assistant professor of psychiatry in the UF College of Medicine.

3 "It's not so much talking on the phone that's typically the problem although that can have consequences[2] too," Merlo said. "(It's) this need to be connected, to know what's going on and be available to other people." According to Merlo, this need is one of the signs of cell phone addiction.

4 Unlike addictions to alcohol, drugs, or even gambling, it can be hard to pinpoint[3] the problems with cell phone use. Almost everyone has a cell phone and uses it regularly. But if someone can't get through dinner without sending text messages, it may be time to take a step back, Merlo said.

5 **Separation Anxiety**

How people respond to being separated from their cell phones is another clue to cell phone addiction. Frequent users often become anxious[4] when they are forced to turn off the phone or if they forget it at home. In fact, these people find that they can't enjoy whatever they're doing unless they have their cell phone on, Merlo

continued

_____

[1] **to interfere (in or with):** to cause problems (in, with, or for)

[2] **consequence:** result or effect of something

[3] **to pinpoint:** to identify or define

[4] **anxious:** nervous and worried

added. Often, cell phone "addicts" cannot stop checking their phones for voice mail and text messages, she said.

6   Cell phone addiction, Merlo continued, is an especially big problem for people who are already anxious or depressed. Their addiction can make their anxiety or depression worse. For example, some people become anxious because their phone calls or messages are not returned right away. These are people who usually already worry about what others think of them.

7 A Growing Problem

The problem seems to be growing. A Japanese study revealed that children with cell phones often don't make friends with children who don't have them. A Hungarian study found that three-fourths of children had cell phones, and an Italian study showed that one quarter of adolescents (young people) owned more than one phone and many claimed to be somewhat addicted to them.

8   A British study also recently found that 36 percent of college students surveyed said they could not get by without cell phones. But this may be more a sign that students view cell phones as a modern necessity like a car, said David

Sheffield, a psychologist who conducted the study at Staffordshire University in England. "The most shocking figure was that seven percent said the use of mobile phones had caused them to lose a relationship or a job," Sheffield said.

9 Signs of Addiction

Although experts have pinpointed these problems in frequent cell phone users, studies do not yet show that a bad cell phone habit is the same as an actual addiction. However, like other addictions, frequent cell phone use is related to certain behaviors. One of these behaviors is using something to feel good. Other behaviors include building up a tolerance for[5] something and needing more of it over time to get the same feeling, and going through withdrawal if deprived of it, Merlo said.

10   Cell phone addiction may start slowly. A cell phone user may replace his first phone with a newer phone. He continues to buy newer and more advanced models because he wants to feel the same pleasure he felt when he bought his first phone, Merlo said.

11   Addiction withdrawal is usually a physical response that happens when the body goes without a chemical. Cell phones, of course,

continued

---

[5] **to build up a tolerance for:** to become less and less affected by something—a drug, medicine, or addictive substance

continued

are not chemicals. However, the anxiety a cell phone user may feel without his phone could simply be another form of withdrawal. If so, frequent cell phone use may be an addiction that shows itself in a different way than an addiction to a chemical substance.

12   Addiction also causes changes in the brain, but scientists have yet to measure what happens in the brains of cell phone users, according to Merlo. Even eating and other behaviors have been shown to produce the same effects in the brain as drugs and alcohol in some people, UF studies have shown.

13 **Solutions**

Frequent cell phone users who think they have a problem can downgrade to a basic phone with fewer features, Merlo advises.

14   "Cell phones are a great technology," Merlo said. "They're useful in a lot of situations. (But) one of the most important things is making sure you have some cell phone free time in your day. It's OK to turn it off. Focus on family, homework, knowing that cell phone message will still be there."

B. Read the text again without pausing. Tell your partner two new things that you remember.

C. Work as a class or in large groups. Try to name as many things as you can about the text.

4 | Understanding the Text

A. Answer as many questions as you can without looking at the text. Discuss your answers with a partner.

1. What can cause anxiety in some frequent cell phone users?

_____

2. For whom is cell phone addiction an especially big problem?

_____

3. How is frequent cell phone use similar to an addiction to a chemical substance?

_____

B. Complete the chart according to the text.

Behaviors that could indicate cell phone addiction
1.
2.
3.

5 | Understanding the Topic, Main Idea, and Supporting Details

A. Text. Answer the questions and discuss your answers with a partner.

1. What is the topic of the text?

   _____

2. What is the main idea of the text?

   _____

3. Are your answers for the topic and main idea here the same as the ones
   you determined after you previewed the text, or are your answers different?

   _____

B. Paragraphs. Answer the questions and write *MI* for *Main Idea* and *SD* for *Supporting Details*. Discuss your answers with a partner.

1. What is the topic of ¶4?

   _____

2. What is the main idea and which are the supporting details for ¶4?

   a. _____ Frequent users often become anxious when they are forced to turn off their
      phone or if they forget it at home.

   b. _____ Often, cell phone "addicts" cannot stop checking their phones for voice mails
      and text messages.

   c. _____ How people respond to being separated from their cell phones is another clue
      to cell phone addiction.

3. What is the topic of ¶6? _____

4. What is the main idea and which are the supporting details for ¶6?

   a. _____ Some people become anxious if their phone calls or messages are not returned
      right away.

   b. _____ Their addiction can make their anxiety or depression worse.

   c. _____ Cell phone addiction is an especially big problem for people who are already
      anxious.

5. What is the topic of ¶9? _____

6. What is the main idea of ¶9? _____

7. What are two supporting details for ¶9? _____

6 | Understanding Vocabulary in Context

A. Collocations. Complete the chart and then fill in the blanks. Discuss your answers with a
partner.

1. Write the correct noun next to each adjective. Then match each collocation with its
   definition.

Adjective	Noun	Definition
_____ 1. modern _____	number	a. a telephone that you can take anywhere
_____ 2. mobile _____	life	b. a number of something that slowly gets bigger over time
_____ 3. growing _____	phone	c. life today

2. Fill in the blanks with the correct collocation from the chart.

a. But for a _____ of people across the globe, the idea of being out of touch…is enough to cause stress.

b. Cellular phones were created to make _____ more convenient.

c. The most shocking figure was that seven percent said the use of _____ had caused them to lose a relationship or a job, Sheffield said.."

B. Context Clues. Select the best meaning for each word or phrase according to the text. Discuss your answers with a partner

1. to claim (¶7)

a. to make

b. to say

c. to grow

2. to be deprived of (something) (¶9)

a. to be without (something)

b. to enjoy (something)

c. to be addicted to (something)

3. to downgrade (¶13)

a. to have difficulties

b. to make a phone call

c. to get something less advanced

7 | Reading Critically

A. Fact and Opinion. Write *F* for *Fact,* and *O* for *Opinion*. Discuss your answers with a partner.

    _____O_____ **1.** Cellular phones were created to make modern life more convenient. (¶2)

    _____ **2.** It can be hard to pinpoint the problems with cell phone use. (¶4)

    _____ **3.** How people respond to being separated from their cell phones is another clue to cell phone addiction. (¶5)

    _____ **4.** A Hungarian study found that three-fourths of children had cell phones. (¶7)

    _____ **5.** Studies do not yet show that a bad cell phone habit is the same as an actual addiction. (¶9)

B. Cause and Effect. Read the following sentences. Label the cause *C* and the effect *E*. Discuss your answers with a partner.

1. "Cellular phones... are actually beginning to interfere in the lives of some users because they don't know when to turn them off." (¶2)

    ____E____ a. Cellular phones are beginning to interfere in the lives of some users.

    ____C____ b. They don't know when to turn them off.

2. "Frequent users often become anxious because they are forced to turn off the phone or if they forget it at home." (¶5)

    _____ a. Frequent users often become anxious.

    _____ b. They are forced to turn off the phone or they forget it at home.

3. "Some people become anxious because their phone calls or messages are not returned right away." (¶6)

    _____ a. Some people become anxious.

    _____ b. Their phone calls or messages are not returned right away.

8 | Discussing the Issues

Answer the questions and discuss your answers with a partner.

1. Do you think cell phone "addiction" could be dangerous? Why or why not?

2. If you thought a friend or family member had a cell phone addiction, what advice (if any) would you give this person?

3. In your opinion, what is the worst effect that a person's cell phone addiction could have on his or her personal relationships?

Putting It On Paper

A. Write a paragraph on one of these topics. You may choose any addiction except the ones mentioned in the chapter.

1. Imagine that you have a friend or family member addicted to a substance. How do you think this addiction would affect your relationship with this person?

2. Imagine that you were addicted to an activity. How do you think this activity would affect your daily life?

Steps for your paragraph

a. In your first sentence, clearly state your topic.

b. In your supporting sentences, use specific examples that will support your opinion about your topic.

c. Be sure to include at least one cause and one effect in your paragraph.

B. Exchange paragraphs with a partner. First, read your partner's paragraph and answer the questions in the checklist. Then give feedback to your partner.

✔ CHECKLIST	
	1. Does the first sentence clearly show which topic your partner chose?
	2. Do the following sentences give examples that support or illustrate the topic?
	3. Does the paragraph show clearly your partner's point of view about his or her topic?
	4. Does the paragraph contain at least one cause and one effect?
	5. Is there any information in the paragraph that is not related to your partner's topic? If yes, please underline it on your partner's paper, and write it below:

_____

_____

_____

_____

_____

_____

_____

C. Revise your paragraph based on your partner's feedback.

Taking It Online | Addictions

A. With a partner, use the Internet to research two addictions.

ONLINE TIP
Many large Websites have their own search engines. Use these search engines to help save time.

1. Use Google (www.google.com) or another major search engine to find Websites with information about two of the following addictions:

   caffeine   gambling

   drugs   smoking

   food   work

2. Preview the Websites.

B. Complete the tables with the information you find.

Addiction 1:
Website address(es):
Describe this addiction:
How is this addiction identified or diagnosed?
What are some treatments for this addiction?

Addiction 2:
Website address(es):
Describe this addiction:
How is this addiction identified or diagnosed?
What are some treatments for this addiction?

C. Following up. Choose one of the addictions. Find a classmate who researched the same addiction, and compare the information you found. Work together to create a brochure about this addiction. Do additional Internet research if necessary.

Vocabulary Index

Skills and Strategies Index

Reading Skills

Previewing

Diagrams, **127**
Graphs and Charts, **11**, 36
Menus and Price Lists, **56**
Newspaper Articles, **46**, 66, 90, 139, 162
Online Articles, Magazine Articles, and Academic
Texts, **4**, 8, 15, 23, 30, 38, 51, 58, 72, 81, 95, 105,
115, 121, 129, 146, 166
Tables, **78**, 172

Reading Critically

Cause and Effect, **77**, 86, 94, 101, 110, 120, 126,
134, 170, 180
Fact and Opinion, **125**, 126, 144, 151, 158, 165,
171, 180

Scanning, 13, 37, 57, 79, 102, 127, 153, 173

Skimming, 145, 146, 154, 174

Understanding

Diagrams, **127**
Graphs, **36**
Main Idea, **69**, 70, 74, 75, 84, 85, 92, 98, 99, 108,
117, 118, 123, 124, 132, 133, 142, 149, 150, 156,
157, 164, 169, 170, 178
Schedules, **102**
Supporting Details, **99**, 108, 118, 124, 132, 133,
142, 149, 150, 156, 157, 169, 170, 178
Timelines, **151**
Topic—Lists, **26**, 33, 41,
Topic—Text and Paragraphs, **27**, 28, 34, 41, 42, 49,
54, 61, 69, 70, 74, 75, 84, 85, 92, 98, 108, 117,
118, 123, 124, 132, 142, 149, 150, 156, 157, 164,
169, 170, 178

Vocabulary Strategies

Skipping Words and Phrases, 3, 8, 15

Understanding

Possessive Adjectives, **100**, 109, 118, 124, 133, 164,
165
Subject and Object Pronouns, **28**, 29, 42, 54, 61,
62, 70, 71, 76, 85
Vocabulary in Context
Collocations, **143**, 150, 157, 158, 178, 179
Context Clues, **119**, 125, 133, 134, 144, 150,
158, 170, 179
Contrasts, **93**, 100, 109, 120, 125, 134
Definitions, **50**, 55, 62, 76, 86, 170
Examples, **71**, 76, 86, 93, 101, 109, 165
Phrasal Verbs, **55**
Synonyms, **35**, 42, 56, 62, 76, 165